Flying
Lure
Fishing

Flying Lure Fishing

With This Book—and This Lure—
You Will Catch More and Bigger Fish
Than You've Ever Dreamed Possible

Alex Langer

NEW YORK

For information address Hyperion, 114 Fifth Avenue,
New York, New York 10011.

Library of Congress Cataloging-in-Publication Data
Langer, Alex.
Flying lure fishing / by Alex Langer.
p. cm.
ISBN 1-56282-800-2
1. Lure fishing. 2. Fishing lures. I. Title.
SH455.8.L36 1994
799.1'2—dc20 93-30506
CIP

Designed by Ann Gold

First Edition

10 9 8 7 6 5 4 3 2 1

To my mother, whose pots and pans I ruined
by melting plastic lures in them

To my father, who took me fishing in the
bitter cold and sleet when he would rather
have been in a warm house

It all worked out.

Contents

Foreword

It was the fall of 1989 when someone told me about "some guy in Boston" who had a unique fishing lure that did what no other lure had ever done. If you had told me at that time that I would go on to be partners with "that guy" in a business whose centerpiece was "that lure," I would have said "you're nuts."

I had never fished, except for one time in Illinois as a seven year old on a farm pond with a bobber. Never caught a fish.

Going into my first meeting with Alex Langer I was as skeptical as they come. Afterward, I was amazed at how excited I was. He was so well-versed on his market that he gave me a crash course in why the Flying Lure was going to be a phenomenal success. He made a believer out of me and I didn't even fish!

His interest in helping fellow fishermen and women catch more and bigger fish is genuine. He loves to hear of people's success out on the water. He loves to hear how people do it. And certainly his biggest thrill is learning of other people's success using the Flying Lure. He revels in it.

If you like to fish, but more important if you like to catch fish, this book will probably do more to add to your success than any other book on fishing techniques that you've read.

Alex's breezy style of writing is how he is in person. He's "real folks," cares about others, and will spend time to find out about others long before you will learn about him.

He sneaks up on you. Just like the Flying Lure.

Read and reread this book. I guarantee you will experience a new level of fishing success that you only dreamed of before, especially if you become a part of the growing Flying Lure family.

Good Luck!

Jim Caldwell

Flying
Lure
Fishing

1

What the Heck Is a Flying Lure?

The Flying Lure Phenomenon

Flying Lure Magic

In a very short time, millions of people around the world have begun using and having success with the Flying Lure fishing system. More people have bought and rebought the Flying Lure in the last year than any other single lure in history. It has set records from the United States to Europe to Australia. Why? Quite simply, because it has helped people, average people, catch more fish and bigger fish than ever before.

A certain mystique has been built up around the lure. In fact, to many people, if it isn't a Flying Lure, it's not a lure. In this book we will look at the Flying Lure phenomenon and will show you why it works and how you can use it to change your fishing life.

The Beginnings of the Flying Lure

In the early dawn hours of December 21, 1991, a half-hour informative TV commercial, or infomercial, broke the silence of the TNN satellite transponder. It was a first in the annals of fishing—a thirty-minute show on *one* fishing lure . . . a single lure! What was so special about this lure to warrant such treatment? Why would anyone care? Who would watch a lure for a half hour? Why would veteran TV producer and host Jim Caldwell call this the most exciting project he's ever worked on? Simply stated, this lure and this TV show were the culmination of over a decade of invention, experimentation, and fishing. Before it was over, it changed the lives of millions of fishermen (or fisherwomen)* forever and turned the fishing industry upside down.

This story began on a small lake, over fifteen years ago, where a nineteen-year-old fisherman was completely frustrated after not catching fish during either day of a two-day bass tournament. This fisherman, who had won his first tournament the previous year, considered himself a hotshot.

But during this tournament, the fish were hiding under heavy brush and floating islands. It was impossible to get a lure to them; the floating islands were too dense to "crash" a lure through and too close to the water to skip a lure under. Although this fisherman was totally frustrated at the end of this tournament, he was determined to catch fish on that lake. He drove home and rigged up a contraption made of several melted plastic worms, a jig, and a piece of a soda can. That fisherman was me.

The Secret of the Flying Lure

I kept the contraption secret for over a decade, telling no one while it was being perfected. Fifteen years later, after intensive research, that contraption turned into the modern Flying Lure, which solved a major problem for millions of fishermen—getting the lure to where the fish are hiding. It went into those places, for the first time, way under cover, where nobody had ever been able to fish before . . . the very *best* places on the lake or ocean.

Not only that, but the lure swam on its own and *fished itself.* The fact that it fished itself and was so easy to use brought in a whole new group of fishermen to the party—those who wanted to fish but didn't know how. People who watched the lure swim on its own for the first time in the water thought it was some kind of trick. How can it do that! They soon found out for themselves. People like James Britton of New Jersey said:

> The TV show sold me, but I was still skeptical on how good it worked. Especially in saltwater. I decided to give the Flying Lure a try in Barnegat

*"Fishermen" is used generically to refer to both men and women.

Jim Caldwell and Alex Langer on the set of the first Flying Lure infomercial. *(Courtesy Jim Caldwell)*

> Bay on the grassy banks. . . . I fished these banks time and again with no luck. I threw everything in the tackle box at them, and nothing! I finally put on the six-inch pearl-color Flying Lure and within minutes had a strike. So I fished for about forty-five more minutes and boated two stripers, one at ten pounds fifteen ounces and an eighteen pound three ouncer . . . both on the Flying Lure.
>
> This is the greatest lure I have ever used. I don't think I will ever use any other lure. Thanks, Alex. You have helped me catch fish and made my wife a believer.

Since the introduction of the Flying Lure, letters like James's have been pouring into our headquarters by the thousands.

Why It's Different

Why is the Flying Lure different from all others? Because it goes in the opposite direction of all other conventional lures. Conventional lures swim toward the angler. The Flying Lure swims away from the angler. So, what's so great about that?

James Britton and his first two striped bass ever that were caught on the Flying Lure. *(Courtesy James Britton)*

What's significant about this unique action is that it captures and "bottles" some incredible benefits for the angler that help catch more and bigger fish. That advantage, coupled with some basic knowledge of how fish behave and where they live, can be an unbeatable combination. Like fisherman Bill Blosser said in the second Flying Lure show, "It helps any fisherman do what only a skilled fisherman could do before." Not only that, but anglers can now do some things that have *never* been possible to do before—with any amount of skill. Some of these benefits are obvious, yet some are very subtle, *and* incredibly important!

Some of the benefits of the Flying Lure system are so subtle that many so-called pros and experts miss them. In fact, they miss the whole concept. We're not just talking about a lure, we're talking about a technique that pushes forward the boundaries of fishing, because it gives fishermen a new tool. This new tool lets the fisherman do the *impossible* according to conventional fishing knowledge. For the angler to gain even greater fishing success than ever possible before, the new knowledge must be identified, named, and used.

In reading this book, you must keep an open mind for many new concepts that I will introduce. These concepts go beyond conventional fishing methods. Many traditional experts and fishermen have a vested interest in maintaining the status quo, since it maintains their position as experts without challenge. The Flying Lure phenomenon is the *first grass-roots fishing revolution* that bypasses many of the conventional "experts" and has been made an overwhelming success by the people themselves. "I've never seen anything like this in twenty-five years in the fishing business," said one leader in the fishing business.

Many innovators and professionals, such as Guido Hibdon, Don Meissner, and Dion Hibdon, and some forward-thinking writers, such as Rich Zaleski and Bill Harnden, saw the benefits of the system early—years ago, when *nobody* knew what a Flying Lure was. When they first realized the possibilities of this system, it was like a jolt of lightning! Many of these people made the lure a way of life, before anyone else did, and gained unparalleled success as a result. I invite you to join this elite group of fishing pioneers that let an open mind lead them to ever greater success.

How the Flying Lure Helps Catch More Fish

The reason that the Flying Lure works so well for so many people is that it takes advantage of a fish's universal habits no matter what time of the year it is, no matter where you are fishing. The fact is, most saltwater and freshwater fish behave in predictable ways—and this includes most species of fish that anglers are seeking.

Tyler Anderson, a fisherman who wrote to me from Arvada, Colorado, discovered for himself that the Flying Lure takes advantage of a fish's predictable wants. Tyler, who fishes offshore and from a boat, has written me several letters. He had been trying to catch trout from his local reservoir, Arvada Reservoir, for *eight* years without success. Since trying the Flying Lure, he has sent us pictures of bass as well as pictures of his *first* trout! Why did he start catching all species as well as trout?

Guido Hibdon catches a nice largemouth bass. *(Courtesy Alex Langer)*

I believe it is because the built-in action of the Flying Lure makes a perfect presentation every time to all species of fish.

Fishing with the Flying Lure takes advantage of what anglers have learned over years of studying and observing fish behavior. Fish hide, eat, and travel in certain ways. They respond to certain stimuli that make them strike out of hunger, anger, and aggression, or reflex response.

The first key to catching fish is to turn a fish's natural hiding instinct, a disadvantage to most fishermen, into an advantage. Fish are great at hiding. Think about it. How many times have you seen game fish frolicking on a sunny, shallow open beach—or basking in the sun? Outside of their spawning time, when nature dictates that fish come shallow, they stay out of the sun as much as possible. Fish camouflage themselves like chameleons, so they're even tough to spot in open water. They take on the color of their surroundings. But they even go beyond that by hiding in the shadiest, most inaccessible places that shield them from the sun and from other fish.

Why are fish such cowards? The underwater world is a dangerous place. It's a war zone. Fish are always in danger of being eaten or hurt by other bigger, more dangerous fish. Bass are afraid of being eaten by other bass, or muskies, or pike. Sunfish are afraid of the bass, and minnows are afraid of the sunfish. So it goes in the food chain. There are no minnows' rights organizations! It's hide or die.

I heard a true story of a monster muskellenge, the world's biggest type of pike, in a small lake in upstate Michigan. This toothy fish was estimated to be ten inches from one eye to the other—measured across the forehead! This musky was probably over five feet long. Whenever this huge fish cruised into a corner of the lake, fishing would stop dead. All the other fish in the area would dive for cover—and stay there until the monster left. This is probably the only fish in the lake that didn't care who saw it. Everyone else was cowering in the shadows. The underwater world works this way.

The other reason most fish hide is that many species are ambush feeders. Most freshwater predators, such as bass and pike, often lay in wait for their prey along the edges of cover. For example, they will lie inside a weed bed facing outward, waiting for another fish to come by. As an unsuspecting fish swims by, the predator surprises the fish and darts out to grab it.

What helps us as fishermen is that these hiding places are both identifiable and predictable. In fact, finding these places is *easy!* I'm

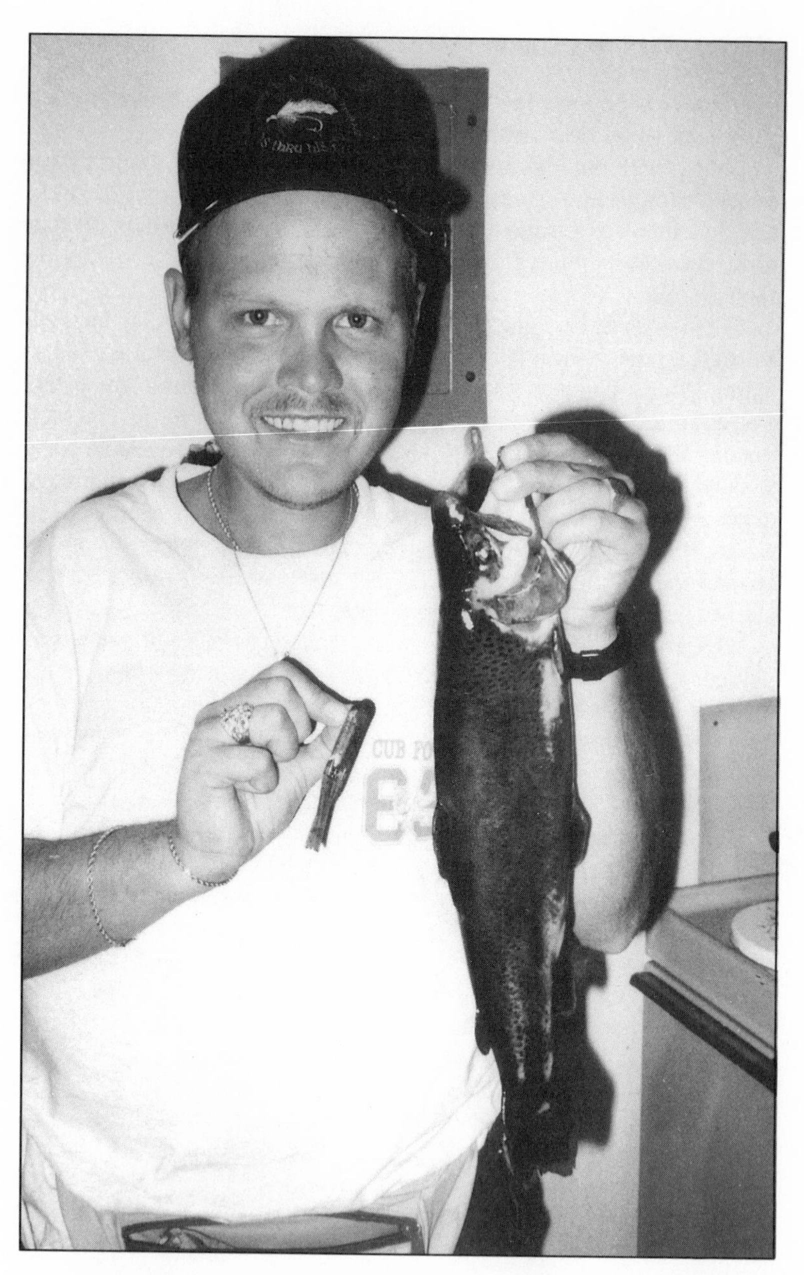

Tyler Anderson and a Colorado rainbow trout. *(Courtesy Stanley Anderson)*

sure you've never been told that anything about catching fish is easy. But that's not true. One of the reasons why so many people have had success with the Flying Lure is because our literature told them *where* to look for the fish. Once you begin to find these places, using the Flying Lure is like mining for gold because it penetrates *inside* these very best places. Nobody has ever done this before in these areas! People have fished near these areas, around these areas, over these areas, but never right *in* these areas. Once you find these areas, a few inches makes a big difference because fish will often not move out of them—not even one inch. You have to go in and get them. Now, with the Flying Lure, you can do just that.

Fishing the Flying Lure in such heavy cover areas satisfies the main motivations of fish while they are in an "undercover ambush" situation. If a fish is hiding, it doesn't have to swim out and expose itself to danger from other fish. It can simply eat the Flying Lure morsel that has meandered into its domain, exerting very little energy to do so, which is always a consideration for a fish. Also, the Flying Lure uses a fish's ambush feeding instinct to an angler's advantage by giving it what it wants—easy prey that lost its way. The key to successful fishing is to understand what the fish wants and to put it where it is hiding.

In Florida, the big bass hide in weed lines and under weeds that form a canopy on the surface of the water. For years in places like Lake Okeechobee, the bait of choice was a live shiner, because these fish, when released, would swim right into the weeds where the bass were hiding. Recently local anglers have begun using six-inch Flying Lure that are colored like live bait (a color called silver shad). These are the first artificial lures that work just like shiners in penetrating the heavy weeds where bass live. Also, being artificial, these lures are easier to use and allow the fisherman to cover more water by making quicker and more casts. Florida fishermen have been having newfound success with the Flying Lure in an area where big bass were caught almost exclusively on live bait.

2

Finding the Secret Places Where Big Fish Hide

The Top Fish Hiding Places

Fish hiding places are all around us. To the untrained eye they are invisible. But to the trained eye of someone who is using the Flying Lure, the sky is the limit. When you use this lure, you'll be able to find them and put your lure right where they live.

There are virgin waters in the midst of busy lakes that receive no fishing pressure, because people don't know about them. Even if they did, they wouldn't have the tools or the knowledge to fish them. Now I'm going to show you how.

Docks

Docks are among the most obvious and seldom-fished areas in a lake or ocean. This is despite the fact that many fishermen stand *on top* of docks and cast *away* from them. They should stop and fish a Flying Lure backward, right *under their feet!*

Famed smallmouth bass angler and TV host Tony Bean tells me of a number of people who have houseboats at his marina on Percy Priest Lake, in Nashville, Tennessee. These folks have begun mopping up on fish by never leaving their houseboats and simply letting the Flying Lure swim itself under the boat dock. They just pull back on the line and let it keep swimming under the dock, over and over, until a fish strikes. In the huge network of docks and piers in that marina, there are hundreds of places that hold fish at certain times. So, save your gas—catch fish at home!

Fish hide under docks because they provide some of the best shade and cover available. Wooden planks stop 100 percent of the light penetration from entering the water, and pilings and pontoons provide hiding places. Even if a dock is busy with people and boats, such as a marina, fish will become used to the activity and hide there anyway.

Some people like to "skip" a lure under a dock by whipping the rod tip horizontally, close to the water, and then releasing the lure. The result is a low-trajectory cast that lets the lure skip across the surface of the water—like a flat rock might. Before I invented the Flying Lure, I used this technique all the time in fishing tournaments. It was, and still is, a great way to place any lure under a dock, provided conditions are right. However, many docks are obstructed by cables and ropes, which, if you skip over, will foul your retrieve and make it impossible to land a fish. Many docks simply don't have any clearance between them and the water. There isn't any space to skip a lure through. This is exactly why the Flying Lure is perfect for this type of cover—you can still get your lure in there without skipping.

If you want to skip, however, the Flying Lure is the best skipping lure ever made. Why? Because it is flat, perfectly balanced, and most of the weight is at the opposite end of the lure from the line. Because of this balance, the lure doesn't twirl in the air, has lots of surface area, and bounces along the water perfectly—two or three times the distance of an average lure. When the lure finally runs out of steam on the surface and sinks, it continues to move away from the angler, providing the ultimate lure for fishing docks.

Skipping is usually done with a spinning reel, which has a fixed spool, and is almost impossible to do with a bait-casting reel. The revolving spool of a bait-casting reel fouls easily and turns the reel into a bird's nest of fishing line. The Flying Lure allows people with bait-casting equipment to penetrate the best areas without skipping.

If you go out and practice fishing docks with the Flying Lure, you will be able to place your lure where others simply cannot. By doing this, you will be fishing in virgin water, right under everybody's nose, and no one will even know it! You will present your lure to big fish that may not have seen a lure that day or in weeks! By doing this, you'll have a much better chance at catching a fish than someone who is fishing "used" water that has been pounded to a froth. The Flying Lure will give you an unfair advantage. Use it!

During a bass fishing tournament on the Merrimack River, which flows through New Hampshire and Massachusetts, I was fishing a large floating dock to which seaplanes were tied. From upstream of the dock, I let a four-inch Flying Lure swim right under the dock. By using the current and pulling and letting go line, I worked the lure twenty feet under the dock. The dock was approximately forty feet wide. Right under the center of the dock, I felt a bump. I set the hook and reeled in a large one-and-a-half- to two-pound crappie—a great fish for that area of the country. I released it and worked my lure under the dock again. Another bump . . . and another crappie of about the same size. This went on for a few more casts, until I got tired of it and had to move on. This was, after all, a bass tournament, and crappie didn't count. What was the lesson here? There was a school of crappie that were unmolested right under the center of that dock! You could have probably caught ten big fish in a row. Why then were people fishing off of that dock, casting into the middle of the river? Who knows? But you should fish the best cover available in an area, even if it happens to be right under your nose. Don't follow the fishless masses.

Although the Flying Lure is perhaps the greatest dock-fishing lure ever designed, please don't use it just for docks. If you do, you'll be missing lots of fish and lots of fun. In many other situations the Flying Lure gives you advantages that no other method does.

Natural Wood Cover: Brush, Trees

Natural wood, such as brush in lakes or flooded trees in reservoirs, is probably my favorite type of cover. It is abundant and holds some of the best fishing in a lake. In fact, the Flying Lure was invented to penetrate just such cover.

A great deal of the letters we get about the Flying Lure involve fishing trees that have fallen in the water. Conventional plastic worms, jigs, and so forth simply cannot do this type of cover justice.

Trae Garrett a fisherman from Henderson, North Carolina, wrote to me of his success with the lure in a sunken tree:

> Dear Masterminds!
> I am so glad somebody finally developed a lure that is original, not a

gimmick and really works!!! It was early February, still winter. . . . I went fishing with a buddy of mine . . . in a farm pond. It had rained all week and was cold, too cold for bass.

There was a tree lying in about four feet of water, so I cast over it and bumped [the lure] up just enough so it would glide under the tree. As I was giving it slack, I saw a huge swirl. At first I thought that I had spooked a turtle or something. But when I saw my line heading out for open water, I tightened up to set the hook. It was an unbelievable pressure . . . my pole was bent over double. I knew it was big, but I didn't realize [how big] until I finally played him out and pulled his head out of the water. I was so nervous with six-pound test line that I stepped into the water and grabbed it. You could have heard me shout for ten miles. The bass weighed nine pounds even, the biggest bass I ever caught in my life. I have never been more excited about the fact that there's a "sure thing" in fishing. Thank you. Thank you. Thank you!

Trae Garrett with his first Flying Lure bass—a nine pounder! *(Courtesy Lisa Garrett)*

What happened to Trae was that the bass was sitting right under that tree because of the prevailing winter conditions. Had Trae pulled a spinnerbait by the tree, he would have probably not caught the fish because cold-water fish tend to be sluggish. He had to put the lure right under the tree—and he did with astounding results.

Often the difference between success and failure in fishing sunken trees can be a few inches—the few inches that a Flying Lure can cover and sail under, right into a lunker's face.

Whitehall Reservoir in Upton, Massachusetts, is notorious among local anglers for having very big bass, some of which are often impossible to catch. These Whitehall lunkers have a formidable fortress to penetrate: floating islands made up of brush and root systems. When the bass are active, they come out from under these matted islands and take conventional lures. When they aren't active, you probably couldn't even get them out with dynamite! They're yards under the brush islands. You can't flip a lure to them or make them come out. At one point, I was so frustrated with these bass, I broke my rod by hitting the side of the boat. Instead of using dynamite, I decided to invent a lure that would go in after the bass, Rambo-style—the Flying Lure.

CRASHING THE BRUSH

Heavy overhanging brush that extends from the shoreline has been the place where I have had the most success. Trees and bushes that grow out over the water form an edge that appears to be the shoreline to many fishermen. Fishermen will cast to within feet or inches of this false shoreline and move on. The real treasure, however, lies feet and yards inside the edge. Fish live and hide underneath these brush canopies, untouched by most anglers—even experienced ones. Often water extends below the limbs and behind them. The real shoreline may be two feet or twenty or more feet beyond where the limbs end.

Crashing the brush is a technique that I invented out of desperation. It is guerilla warfare when it comes to catching fish. No sane human would try it. People scratch their heads in disbelief when they first see it. Using a heavy-action spinning rod and twelve- to seventeen-pound test line, you look for openings in the limbs, not near the surface of the water, but above it. Let's say you see an opening of one foot in diameter in the brush that is facing you, but it's six feet above the water level. What do you do? You cast your lure into the opening, of course. Most fishermen would never do this because they fear losing their lure. Even if you catch a fish, you would never get it out of there—right? Well, actually you *are* right . . . but the trick is to go in after that fish and not to pull it out.

Here's how one experience in crashing worked. It was nearly dusk (my favorite time of the day). All of the other fishing boats on the lake had already gone back to the launch ramp. One stretch of brush in this particular lake is awesome. It has major trees stretching thirty feet over the water. As usual, I was casting a four-inch Flying Lure into openings above the water and letting it sink into the water below to swim even farther on its own. This lure had a stiff fiber weed guard, although you can use a soft plastic weed guard for fishing the brush as well. The legs on a Flying Lure act as a natural weed guard and flip the hook away from branches most of the time.

I made a cast over a large clump of limbs six to seven feet above the water and let the lure descend, then plop into the water. At once, I heard a splash behind the brush and felt a bump on the line. It is important to listen to what is happening in such a situation. Often your sense of feel through the fishing line is diminished since it is hanging over limbs and can't transmit a fish's taps or motion as well as an unobstructed line can. I gave the lure some slack line for one to two seconds, to make sure that the fish really had a good hold of it. Then, reeling in as much slack line as possible, I set the hook. The water behind the limbs exploded with a tremendous splashing and churning. My line strained. The branches over which I had cast were bending under the weight of a huge fighting fish. The fish swam right, then left. I just tried to hold it, giving it some slack so my line wouldn't pop. After several minutes of this, I was able to get the fish's head out of the water, just beyond the gills. Now came the task of actually going in to get it. I put the electric trolling motor on high speed and pointed it toward the clump of limbs where I was holding my quarry. The trick in going in to get the fish is to keep its head out of the water while moving the boat in toward shore. This is an interesting balancing act—coordinating the speed of the boat with line intake so the line doesn't break or allow the fish's nose to slip back below the surface. If its head slips back in the water, it has a chance to break free again. This maneuver takes some practice.The fish was actually six to eight feet past the edge of the brush line. The bow of the boat crashed through the trees. I had to dodge the limbs and control the boat and the rod at the same time. All of this commotion made the fish start to act up again, but I was able to keep its head above the water. Leaning down through the brush, I made a grab for the fish's lower jaw and succeeded on the first try. A heavy eight-pound six-ounce bass grudg-

Alex with a giant bass caught in brush. *(Courtesy Alex Langer)*

ingly came out of the water. There was no way that the fish was coming out of there the same way the lure went in. I cut my line and released my rod, which was now firmly entangled in the trees. Was it easy to catch that fish? No! Was it better than not catching a fish at all? Yes, a thousand times over. I have relived that story many times and will remember it all my life.

What is the lesson here? Simply do what no others do. Go the extra mile. Find the very best places in the brush and figure out a way to fish them. The best fish hide in the best, densest brush and overhangs, not in easy-to-get-to twigs. And . . . don't be afraid to lose lures! I'm not just saying this because I make lures . . . honest! I am constantly amazed how people will spend $20,000 on a boat, $1,000 on rods and reels, $100 on oil and gas to go fishing for the weekend, and then be frightened about losing a $1 lure. Plan to lose lures. I would routinely lose $20 to $50 per day or more in lures just to place them in the best areas where others wouldn't dare. This often makes the difference between great fishing and so-so fishing. Don't skimp where it counts.

Weeds

In many lakes, especially natural lakes, weeds are the key to locating and catching fish. Weeds such as lily pads are obvious places to fish a Flying Lure since they provide cover on the surface. You can fish the lure over the tops of the weeds with an exposed hook because the lure's design makes it always ride upright on the surface of the water. When you reach the edge of the pads, or an opening, you can let the lure drop inside the opening and actually swim under the weeds it just swam *over!* In top-water situations such as lily pads, you get a lot of missed strikes. You can release the Flying Lure to go back after those missed strikes without recasting by simply giving the lure some slack line. This is a real time-saver during those critical seconds when a fish is near your lure and interested in it—ready to hit it again because it's mad that it just missed it!

The first time he used it on his home lake, Gary Lubarsky used the Flying Lure to swim under some weeds near deep water. The result? The biggest bass of his life! Now his wife also fishes with Gary!

Matted weed beds are great hiding places for bass in most lakes and reservoirs. Matted weeds are heavy clumps of weeds that grow toward the surface of the water and often lay on the surface, forming a canopy. Fish hide under these shady canopies. Guido Hibdon, Dion Hibdon, and I were fishing a bay in a large canal in the late summer. Clumps of matted weeds were growing in four to six feet of water, interspersed with lily pads. In one of those rare days when you can say you got the lead in a ball game with Babe Ruth, I caught four fish before Guido and Dion had their first one. While Guido took it with good humor, he was not happy! He wanted to see what I was doing.

I was casting beyond the clumps of weeds, which were two to six feet in diameter, and bringing the lure over the weeds like a spoon. The open

Gary Lubarsky with his biggest bass ever (over eight pounds)—caught the first time he used the Flying Lure. *(Courtesy Martha Lubarsky)*

hook was riding over the weeds unobstructed because it had already aligned itself in an upright position when I began to retrieve it in open water, before it reached the weeds. After I pulled the lure over the clump of weeds, I let it go right into and under it. Fish that were interested in the lure when it got their attention on the surface were hitting it when it was released into their domain. It didn't take Guido and Dion long to catch on. Soon they were neck and neck with me. Bass fisherman Pat

Roy, who was my fishing partner, ended up catching the lunker of the day.

Bass love weeds. They live in them and make them their home among them. Find weeds that are in fertile food shelves, such as the one we were fishing, or weed beds near deep water. The Flying Lure is especially weedless (it can shield its hook from catching on underwater weeds and other obstructions) because of the way it is designed. The legs act as a natural weed guard during the retrieve. Also, it does not sink into a weedy bottom and become tangled, like a jig. Because of its wide footprint, it rests on a weedy bottom like a snowshoe, ready to be retrieved without picking up muck along the way.

The Flying Lure is also great for fishing deep weed lines because of its slow fall and weedless ability. I routinely fish the lure in ten to twenty feet of water, swimming it into weed beds and around weed lines. I fish the Flying Lure right under the boat on one of my favorite lakes, on top of a seventeen-foot-deep point. This point has a great weed bed right on its edge that holds an excellent population of bass in the summertime. By the way, this point is just 200 feet straight out from the launch ramp. While boats are whizzing by, I'm catching fish by letting the lures swim along the weed bed, seventeen feet straight down. The water-skiers and other fishermen must think, "What a dummy! Why doesn't he go find some fish?" as they speed by. I say again, "Why waste gas?" You'll learn more about finding these deep-water areas when I discuss the Flying Lure fishing system later in the book.

Finding and Fishing the Best Bottom Obstructions

Bottom obstructions are features of the lake, river, or ocean bottom that provide housing to fish. I call fish that hide here cave dwellers. "Caves" where fish hide include riprap (crevices between rocks used to build bridge abutments and highway supports), culverts or pipes that run into a body of water, crevices in a rock jetty, bluffs with ledges, or undercut banks in rivers and streams.

Amaze Your Friends with the Culvert Trick

One example of cave-dwelling fish that I often catch live in a culvert on a small lake near my home. This lake is a joggers' paradise. Urban-dwelling yuppies and pesky dog owners can be seen running around its banks day and night. Lots of urban fishermen give this lake fishing pressure with live bait and lures of all kinds. There's nothing that these fish haven't seen.

A small culvert feeds this lake with water from another lake. This culvert is in a highly trafficked area. People are constantly fishing around it. A trick I often perform when I get bored on a Sunday afternoon is to drive up to the lake in my car and park a few feet away from the culvert. Then I ceremoniously take out my single fishing rod with one lure tied on . . . usually a four-inch Flying Lure. I carry no tackle box. I walk to the culvert and lean over it. To either side of it, there are granite lips that have a one- to two-foot overhang. Fish love this place! The moving current sweeps minnows and other food past here and the bass are protected from the sun and other predators. I make my first "cast"—an underhand lob to the edge of the rock culvert—and work the lure inside of it. I feel a bump and set the hook. Out comes a two- to three-pound bass, which I unhook and release. I make my second cast, another bump, and this time a bigger bass comes leaping out of the water. By now I have their attention. All the other fishermen on the bank are watching me. I make my third cast, work the lure a little bit, and get a third hit. The hook is set and yet another fish breaks the surface of the water. Three casts . . . three fish. By now people are walking over to watch what's happening. At that point I release the fish, put my lure away, smile, walk back to my car, and drive away. Some are left scratching their heads, asking "Who was that man?"

Find the Hidden Cave Dwellers

There are underwater caves made by humans and by nature that are unseen from the surface. But . . . if you know what you are looking for, you can find them and catch hidden fish.

NATURAL CAVES

Undercut banks are formed in rivers and streams when water washes against an earth bank and erodes the earth a little bit at a time. After a while caves form underneath the bank, below the surface of the water. These caves are perfect hiding places for fish. As the water washes away these undercut banks, the roots of trees growing on top of them are exposed and form hiding places. They are like upside-down trees growing from the roof of the undercut bank that provide shelter and break up the water current. Fish of all kinds, and especially trout, are notorious for hiding in these places. I have actually seen people in Europe wading in streams without a fishing rod or net to catch these fish. They come right up to an undercut bank and reach their arms inside the tangle of roots under the bank. After a few moments of grappling and wrestling, the person brings out a live and kicking brook trout! If I hadn't once seen this myself, I wouldn't have believed it. I witnessed a man who caught six fish in a few minutes by going from root system to root system along the undercut banks of the stream using nothing but his bare hands . . . illegally, I might add. Even though this man had lost several fingers on one hand in an industrial accident, he was still able to catch the fish with incredible dexterity. Or maybe it wasn't an industrial accident—maybe he tried it in Florida once and ended up with a 'gator.

Fortunately, you can catch these same fish in the root systems of undercut banks easily and *legally!* Unlike other lures, the Flying Lure can penetrate these areas via horizontal underwater motion. This is exactly the action you need *both* to go under the bank and to swim through the roots to reach the fish. Using the two-inch Flying Lure in dark, natural colors is a deadly technique, especially in small trout streams. For bass and larger fish use the four-inch or six-inch models—and use the weed-guard option. Either use jigheads with the fiber weed guard attached, or at least engage the soft weed guard available on every Flying Lure. You use the soft weed guard by impaling the middle tail strand of the lure on the hook, past the barb, and impaling the other end of the strand on the lead clip on the top rear of the lure body. The weed guard will deflect the especially pesky roots in these underwater labyrinths.

Let your lure work itself under the bank and into the roots. Just give it line while it is sinking and swimming forward. Once the line stops moving, give it a slight pull and let it go forward again. Don't do too much. Let the lure fish itself. Work it in one place. Tease the fish. Be ready for the slightest bump on your line. It's probably a good fish. I have found that fish in undercut banks tend to be larger specimens, compared to fish in less ideal locations, because undercut banks are choice real estate. Food is swept by here all the time by the water current. It's a fish buffet, and it's free—with a nice atmosphere to boot! Bigger fish get the best hiding places. Also, these fish tend to be more aggressive than average because they are so well hidden from the light and current and feel secure.

Look for undercut banks wherever a river or stream takes a turn. The outside bank—the one against which the water is rushing—will usually be eroded if it is made of relatively soft earth. Even if the bank is made of hard rock, the banks that take the brunt of the water current's force tend to be the better ones, since food is always being swept by. Even if there is no undercut in the bank, eddies (quiet places) are formed by rock outcroppings, crevices, or debris in the water. Fish will also hide in these quiet areas with a slow current and wait for their meal to come by.

HIDDEN FISH IN BLUFFS AND CREVICES

Usually bluffs are rock cliffs made of shale or sandstone that is eroded over time. These cliffs have a multitude of crevices and overhangs where fish can hide.

Tony Faria, a friend of mine, uses the Flying Lure to fish the bluffs of an old flooded rock quarry. He fishes out of a small johnboat and simply pitches the lure against the rock walls with short casts. Says Tony:

> When I'm fishing against the bluffs . . . I cast toward them and bounce the lure down [the face of the bluff]. The entire time [it's sinking], it's bouncing away from me up against the wall. . . . I draw it back a little bit and let it fall. As it falls away from you, just keep working it down, and it will actually go up underneath ledges and overhangs.

In this short quotation, Tony has revealed the keys to fishing bluffs: Keep the lure right next to the face of the wall, don't let it swim away from the wall like conventional lures, and let it swim under the ledges. That's it. Simple. This style of fishing has never been possible before! The Flying Lure greatly increased the success rate of many people who fish reservoirs in the South and West that are replete with bluffs and rock walls. While the Flying Lure is not magic, it *is* a better tool to fish this type of situation.

Fish generally will suspend somewhere along the face of a bluff or will hide under the rock outcroppings. Take a look at a natural rock wall when you're driving down a road sometime. There are hundreds of irregularities, undercuts, and crevices. Now imagine that wall underwater. Fish will use the features of that wall to hide and find food.

PIPES, BARRELS, AND SUBMERGED OPENINGS

Any area underwater that has shade and is segregated from the open water has the possibility of being a fish-holding area. Such areas provide the shelter that fish seek as well as a place from which to ambush prey. A great hidden variation on the culvert, or small bridge, is the submerged culvert. Watch for these whenever the water level is low. They can be nothing more than a small pipe that enters the water, or they can be a larger opening such as a runoff drain or a small bridge over a stream running into a lake. Once you spot them at low water, these places can be an undiscovered gold mine that only you know about.

Cast toward these areas and let your lure bounce down the vertical face of the wall, which is usually around the opening. The beauty of the Flying Lure in this case is that it will bump along the wall face until it reaches the hole. Then it will swim inside on its own power—because the lure is always trying to go forward. Keep giving the lure slack line as it tries to find the crevice. Once it does so, it will begin taking line a little bit faster than before. This happens because the lure is no longer scraping along the surface of the wall but traveling ahead unimpeded. Pay very close attention to your line once it begins coming off the spool more quickly. This means that the lure has entered the opening and is swimming more quickly. Usually fish will be right at the mouth of the opening. Once the lure swims through, the more aggressive fish usually hit. Keep working the lure in one place inside the opening, teasing the less aggressive fish if necessary.

Any pipe running into the water could hold a fish—either inside or beside it. You can often see pipes on shore running into the water. Find where they end in the water and you may have yourself a hot spot.

Barrels and tires are oddball types of cover that often hold fish overlooked by others. They are perfect cover for the Flying Lure fisherman, who can penetrate them. Fishing tournaments in urban areas often have an abundance of such cover. A "tire bass" has put me in the money more than once!

The most unusual place in which I ever caught a bass in these man-made caves was a discarded washing machine. My tournament partner was mad at me for fishing such a stupid piece of cover and began to pull the boat away against my protests. After a few twitches with the Flying Lure, a two-and-a-half-pound bass came jumping out of the washing machine—hooked on my line! My partner was absolutely dumbfounded. I'm sure that nobody else in that tournament would lower themselves to fish that white enamel piece of cover either. That washing machine bass put us in the money! You might say it was a clean finish.

RIPRAP

Riprap is a term used to describe rock walls that descend into the water from the sides of a road or a bridge. Riprap is made of stones that generally have a flat surface and are two to five feet across. Between the rocks, there are crevices that hide food for game fish, such as crayfish and minnows. Bass tend to hover near certain areas of riprap where they feed on the creatures that hide in the crevices. If the riprap is in a reservoir or a river, the irregular stones create eddies in current. Let your lure bounce down the face of the riprap. Work it back and forth, like a crawfish scooting back into cover after being pulled out. Since the lure stays right next to the cover, it remains in the strike zone all the time, all the way down the bank.

Pay particular attention to places where there is any irregularity in the riprap, including any change in the size of the stones. Many times bass will be near the irregular stone, whether it is larger or smaller than the surrounding rock. Any weeds or fallen timber on top of the riprap can be fish magnets that you can "sail" your Flying Lure under. Wherever the riprap takes a turn is an area to check out. Inside turns—that is, turns where riprap forms a U—are often excellent. The bottom near a U often gets shallower and forms a food shelf, sometimes even with a solitary weed patch. If you find an area like this, surrounded by deep water, look out! It is a prime feeding area where game fish will feed on minnows hiding in the weeds or debris.

Another key area in the riprap is where it meets the deepest water or an open channel. Under a bridge, the areas on either side of it, where the riprap ends, are generally the very best. Outside of each side of the riprap, the rocks turn to form a point. Fish often camp out at each of the four possible points, because the water flows by there. These points form natural resting points when fish are traveling through riprap channels. They are also natural ambush points for big fish to wait for minnows to swim by.

Cast your lure near these edges and let the current sweep it past the riprap. If there is no current, simply cast to either side of the edge. If there is an obstruction near the edge, or even within yards of it, pay particular attention. A sunken tree or a patch of weeds close to edges of riprap can be productive staging areas because of their difference from the vast expanse of riprap that usually surrounds them.

Don Meissner and Alex Langer fish a bridge with pilings and riprap while shooting a TV show. *(Courtesy Jim Caldwell)*

Riprap is often overlooked, but it can pay big dividends if you know what you are looking for.

JETTIES

Jetties are rock peninsulas that are usually found in salt water and in larger freshwater lakes, or freshwater seas. They are man-made and provide a barrier to protect beaches and harbors from the waves and tides. Jetties are also great places for fishing and recreation. The rocks that make up jetties are often large—three to six feet in diameter.

Jetties are a rich feeding ground for many species of fish. Baitfish hide between the rocks, drawing larger fish. Shellfish and other mollusks make their home among the rocks and are a rich food source.

Use Flying Lures to penetrate the vast areas between the rocks that hold fish of all kinds. Don't just cast away from the jetty as far as you can, as most people do. Sometimes the best piece of cover in the whole area is the jetty itself.

Before I invented the Flying Lure, I used to fish with live bait straight down from jetties and saltwater piers, and catch as many fish as those who were casting as if their lives depended on how far they cast. Use the currents to swim the Flying Lure in and around the rocks. Don't do too much. Let the lure work itself as it is bouncing along and among the rocks. Use it as you would live bait. Have confidence that the fish will eat it and hang onto it. Always watch your line. Catch those overlooked fish that have probably moved into the rocks to avoid the steady barrage of lures farther out.

Fishing for Spawning Bass

Some of the most incredible experiences I have ever had are those in the spring, fishing for spawning fish. At this time, warm-water species of fish, such as largemouth and smallmouth bass, panfish, and others, build circular nests in relatively shallow water in which to deposit their eggs and reproduce. Bass protect their nests and will generally attempt to attack or remove any foreign visitors (a.k.a. lures).

Recently I took a fishing trip to New Hampshire, to the lake on which the film *On Golden Pond* (with Henry Fonda and Katharine Hepburn) was made. The real "Golden Pond," Squam Lake, is a classic New England retreat with fishing cabins, colorful local characters, and small-town New England charm. The lake is pristine, with super-clear water. On a calm day, you can see ten to twenty feet straight down! I went there with a New England bass fishing club called the Mass Masters to do some field-testing of the Flying Lure.

This was a perfect testing ground because you could see exactly what the lure was doing at all times. You could also see how the fish were reacting to the lure. It was almost like fishing in an aquarium.

I was fishing with my good friend Ray Lentine, a longtime outdoor radio talk show host heard in Massachusetts. Ray has been fishing this lake for decades and was my guide. We were spotting and fishing smallmouth beds in five to twelve feet of water. We would cast a Flying Lure toward the bed and let it sink beyond it. Then we would work the lure toward the bed by lifting the rod tip a few inches and letting the lure swim forward to the bottom again. This proved to be an absolutely deadly technique. Bass on or near beds need to be teased. They will not strike a lure that passes by them quickly during the spring. They will, however, try to kill anything that repeatedly invites itself onto their bed—as the Flying Lure does repeatedly by swimming back in their faces. Time after time, the fish did not hit the lure at once. They would hit it only after being teased three, four, five, or ten times!

This experience brought to mind the now-famous sequence from the Flying Lure infomercial where a smallmouth bass is enticed into taking the lure after seeing it go back in its face multiple times. This happens all the time with this lure . . . and not just in the spring. Neutral or nonfeeding fish need to be coaxed into striking. This is where the concept of *persistence* comes in. We'll discuss persistence in Chapter 9. Most fish are not feeding most of the time. You need to be persistent and coax them into striking. Conventional lures are not made to be persistent. Once you retrieve conventional lures past a fish, they're gone, never to be seen by that fish again. You've lost the opportunity to keep that lure working in the strike zone, close to cover.

Going back to our experiences on "Golden Pond," if the fish swiped at and missed our lures, we would simply let them glide back toward the fish—and let the fish hit them again. I also firmly believe that changing a lure's direction during the retrieve is a definite strike trigger. For years fishermen have observed that a fish strikes the lure just at the moment a crankbait or a spinnerbait changes direction. This is usually accomplished by changing the angle of the rod from side to side or bumping the lure against an obstruction, such as a rock or a log. I cannot prove it, but I think that the greater the angle of change in the retrieve, the greater the strike trigger it is. The greatest strike trigger possible, in my opinion, is a 180-degree turn in the lure's direction. Through underwater tests and filming in many environments I have proved to my own satisfaction that making a lure go back into a fish's face is the most strike-provoking action any lure can take. Doing this multiple times is as close to a sure-fire method as I have ever seen. It is almost unfair.

Club members noticed another key item about fishing the spawn. Of all the lures used over three days, the Flying Lure was the only one that many fish would actually swim off their beds to attack—the first time they saw it. They did not pay any attention to conventional jigs until the jig was right in the center of the nest. I believe that this was due to the completely natural swimming action of the Flying Lure—unimpeded by human error in the retrieve. Jigs and other lures either swam by the nest too quickly, never to return, or sank quickly, like a stone. This also explains why many people report that they consistently get more hits with the Flying Lure at all times of the year. It's just as you see in the tank in the Flying Lure TV infomercial. Those fish went wild over the Flying Lure while only sporadically touching others. With these soft plastic lures, the fall is the most important part of the retrieve. Other lures are not engineered to take full advantage of it with a natural side-to-side motion and a slow programmed fall.

Catch and Release

Whenever possible, I support the catch and release of all species of fish. In my book, a valid exception to catch and release is whenever fish will be used immediately and responsibly for food—not hoarded for the sake of hoarding. There's nothing wrong with keeping fish to eat. It's right, it's healthy, and it's delicious! In fact, lakes benefit from an intelligent harvest of fish. Underfished ponds can become overpopulated with small, stunted fish. I have fished ponds like this, where you can catch hundreds of bass every day, all six to ten inches long. Due to a population explosion, food becomes scarce, leaving a lot of small fish to fight for a little food. Fish are a resource to be used responsibly, admired, and restored, not to be wasted or mythologized.

Here's how the mechanics of catch and release really work. When using lures with a single hook, such as the Flying Lure, fish are usually hooked in the area of the mouth cartilage, a hard, resilient mass. There aren't even blood capillaries here. Puncturing this area is much like clipping your fingernail.

I feel most strongly about catch and immediate release when you are fishing in the spring. During spawning time, fish reproduce and some, such as bass, protect their nests full of eggs. It is appropriate to remove a fish from its parental duties if you see it come off a nest. If you catch a fish during the spawn, release it as quickly as possible, as close to where you caught it as possible.

Some people may keep an occasional big fish in the spring. That's okay. I don't think that, with conventional fishing methods, humans can ever fish out a lake or river. But they will make the population of fish move to protect itself. Fish will simply move away from fishing pressure—either deeper or toward a portion of a lake that is not "pounded" by anglers.

Tournament anglers are sometimes challenged with respect to fishing for spawning fish. Guido Hibdon, a Bass Masters Classic winner, once asked a critic of fishing for spawners at a seminar, "Do you fish between February and June?" The vociferous critic replied, "Of course I do!" "Then," said Guido, "you're a hypocrite because you're fishing for spawning fish and you don't even know it!" Guido was right. Unless we completely stop fishing in the spring and early summer, we are, by definition, fishing for spawners. Simply stated, we must have balance in our fishing, not black-and-white rules. Use your informed judgment. Protect what you have, or one day it will be gone.

3

How to Fish the Flying Lure

The Flying Lure is a very simple lure to use. It is programmed to fish itself—by design.

Three-and-a-Half-Year-Old Outfishes Dad and Catches a Lunker!

Randy Niquette of upstate New York wrote to me about the effectiveness of the Flying Lure's slow preprogrammed action in teaching his young son, Scott, to fish. He writes:

> . . . To be quite honest, I never used [Flying Lures] much. Then one day I was fishing with my son, Scott, who was about three and a half years old at the time. I caught a few bass, and he wanted to catch something bigger than panfish. But he wasn't old enough to understand how to use a jig and pig, so he opened up my tackle box and picked up a Flying Lure and said he wanted to use it. Well, he did and enclosed is a picture of my son's first largemouth bass, and yes, it was caught on the Flying Lure. This fish was almost twenty-four inches long and weighed close to seven pounds. I was amazed, but thought it was just luck. Scott continued to catch more and bigger fish than me for about two more hours. Then I switched to the Flying Lure.

The Flying Lure's natural fish-catching action is often overlooked in the presence of other, more "striking" benefits, such as going under cover. However, some of the lure's most potent fish-catching ability lies in this action. Unfortunately, the words natural, fish-catching, and action have been so overused by everyone in the lure business as to have become meaningless. You just have to see the lure work. The Flying Lure is unique in that it is the only lure to require *no* human actions *whatsoever* during its descent. This allows the lure to be a completely natural body in its environment, interacting with water currents, bouncing off and going around obstructions, and so forth. Never at any point is the lure's descent flawed by human error.

It is we humans, not fish, who think lures need to be overworked in an exaggerated manner. It's like bad acting! The fish are probably

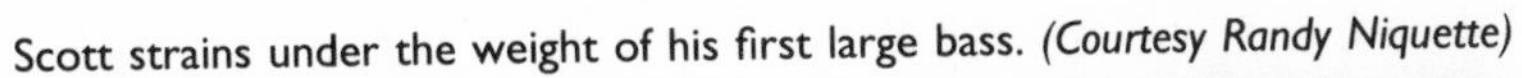
Scott strains under the weight of his first large bass. *(Courtesy Randy Niquette)*

laughing at the amateur actors that most lures are, trying to mimic what should be subtle, fluid, and almost motionless gliding, by jerking, darting, and other sorts of buffoonery. After I fished with four-time world champion bass angler Rick Clunn, and showed him how to use the lure for the first time, he astutely observed that "most of us [fishermen] haven't learned how to stop cranking the reel." Rick is so right! Less is more. It's easy to teach a three-and-a-half-year-old like Scott to just raise and lower his rod tip and let the lure do the rest. He's eager to learn and has no ego tied up in pet methods. Therefore he's much easier to teach than an opinionated "expert" who is set in his ways. Some people will just never get it . . . and that's okay. Remember: Less is more. Fish are what counts, not ego. Little egos catch big fish, because they're always willing to learn.

If you look at the lure closely, it is divided into two basic parts, the body and the tail. The body is a unique planing surface. If you look at it from the side, the nose looks like the leading edge of an airplane wing. The soft body is made to interact with the jighead to provide lift in the water and to make the whole lure glide forward and pull the line behind it. Believe it or not, that simple design took years to perfect. The patent attorneys who worked on the project stated that many of the formulas used on the lure were similar to the concepts used in human-powered aircraft. The idea in both cases is to make a wobbly, nonrigid body "fly" through its respective medium.

The ability of the lure to fly through the water, however, is not enough. A natural action must be coupled with it. The interaction of the tail with the shape of the body gives the Flying Lure its characteristic side-to-side swimming motion. This motion combined with the slow fall inherent in the lure's flying action gives it its unique fish-catching action. The lure performs this action entirely on its own. And it is this action, which the lure has every time it is released, that gives it its unique appeal in open water or under cover.

Is Instant Success Possible?

The self-propelled swimming action of the Flying Lure is what enables a child like Scott Niquette to catch a lunker bass. In my estimation, it takes at least six months of fishing to learn how to use a plastic worm or a jig properly, not expertly, just properly. The Flying Lure will perform perfectly on the first cast, as well as it will on the thousandth cast. Using the lure requires much less manual dexterity than using conventional lures.

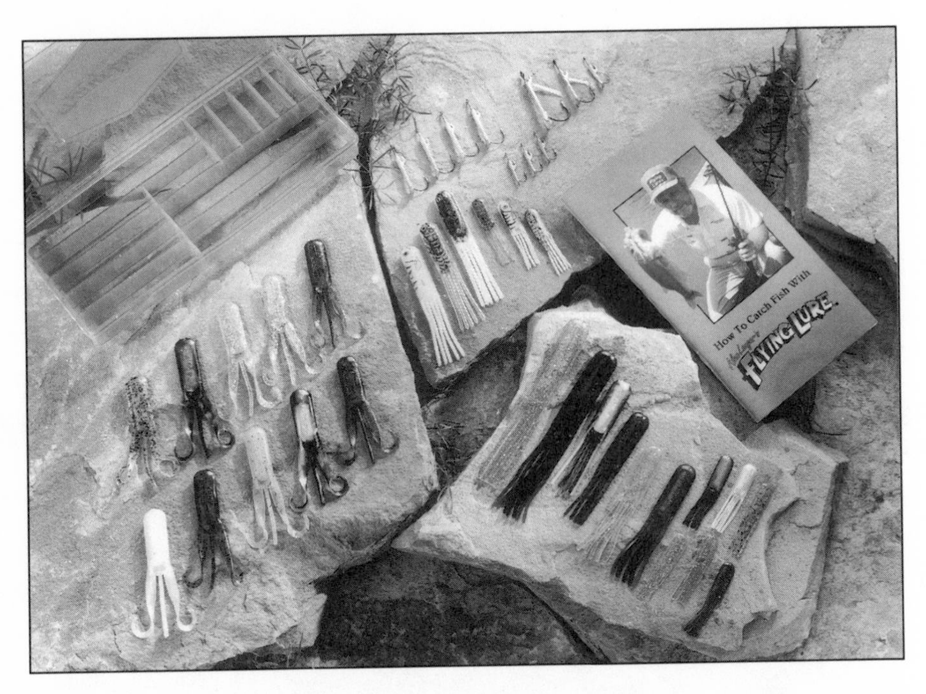

A sampling of Flying Lures. Crawtails, Glidin' Naturals, Jigheads and the original Flying Lures. *(Photo © Future Thunder Productions)*

Don Meissner's Secret to Fishing the Flying Lure

Don Meissner, host of the TV show *Rod and Reel Streamside* on public television stations, was the first major figure to discover the Flying Lure. Since his discovery, he probably has caught more fish on the lure than anyone else . . . except me.

Don and I first met at the national fishing trade show, AFTMA (American Fishing Tackle Manufacturers' Association), when I was just starting to market the Flying Lure. I had a tiny little booth, with a thirty-gallon aquarium as a demonstration tank. My friend Paul Martinez was helping me with the booth as a favor. That aquarium is where Paul and I first demonstrated the lure to Don and Guido and Dion and Rick Clunn, and to anyone else who would watch.

When I tried the lure in the Hawg Trough (a huge tank that contained

Don Meissner, host of *Rod and Reel Streamside.* *(Courtesy Jim Caldwell)*

live bass) for the first time, it caused a stir at the show. Actually, women's professional fishing champion Linda England tried it. She caught five fish on five casts—and then took it off her line. I continued to "mop up" for three days! Viewers were stunned. That started the tradition of fish tearing up the lure in a tank in front of hundreds of spectators watching—when other lures were not performing! But more on that later.

Don liked the concept of the lure but didn't really try it until months later. He was having a tough time catching fish one day and said, "What the heck, I'll try it!" Well, he started catching all kinds of species of fish, on TV, when no other methods would work. He became a believer first and then the world's foremost expert on the use of the Flying Lure. What he can do with the lure is incredible. He fishes the lure in open water, he drifts with it, he even trolls it. He does everything that I haven't thought of—and I invented it! In writing this book, I went to Don first and asked what the secret to fishing the Flying Lure was. Don's answer was deceptively simple, yet profound. He said, the secret to fishing the Flying Lure is to do nothing.

The Flying Lure is introduced at our first AFTMA trade-show booth. Paul Martinez demonstrates the Flying Lure. *(Courtesy Ken Pripepass)*

Don Says Don't Do Anything

According to Don, the Flying Lure depends on your doing nothing! That's right . . . absolutely nothing. Most educated fishermen can't accept that. The Flying Lure depends on you simply giving the lure enough slack line so it can work itself, as it was designed. That's it. When the lure has landed on the bottom, lift your rod tip to give it a new starting point, so it can swim again, on its own. Give it some slack line and it's off. That's it. That's why anyone can catch a fish on it.

This lure will catch fish on its own. Don thinks of it as *unfishing.* That is, you're not doing the fishing, the lure is. All you are doing is controlling the starting point of the lure's next glide to the bottom.

Don feels that the reason some experienced fishermen may have trouble fishing the lure is because all other lures depend on the fisherman having to do *something.* Crankbaits need to be reeled, plastic worms need to be hopped and worked. Consequently, many experienced fishermen try to fish the lure too hard. They give it fast, violent motions. They don't give it any slack line. They reel it and twitch it, just as if it were a conventional lure . . . *wrong!* It never has a chance to work this way. This lure works when you're not—always remember that.

Casting the Lure

The Flying Lure doesn't really need to be cast in the traditional manner. If you are right next to cover, such as a dock or a tree, you can simply dangle the lure in the water and let it glide away from you by giving it slack line. To give the lure direction, give it a slight pull away from the direction you want it to go. For example, if you want it to go under a dock, let the lure hang off your rod tip and suspend in an inch or two below the surface of the water. Then pull it *away* from the dock about a foot. As you pull it away, the lure will align itself in a hook-up position and will be pointed directly at the object you want to penetrate. Then simply let it go by giving it slack line. The lure will swim in its intended direction—away from the direction in which you have pulled it. The fishing line acts as a tail on a kite might. It helps the lure achieve proper direction and stability in its glide path.

You can also cast the lure in a conventional manner, toward the cover you want to penetrate. Let's say that you're casting at a stump and want to have the lure bounce down and penetrate its roots underneath. Make your normal overhand cast and let the lure hit the water and sink on a slack line. The bait will simply continue its cast underwater and will right itself and continue to swim forward.

If you want the lure to make a soft landing in the water to minimize the splash when fish are spooky, simply stop the line with your hand when the lure is about a foot over the water and about to land. This will stop the lure short of its target. The lure will lose its momentum and settle softly in the water. Pull the lure toward you a few inches after it lands, to give it the proper orientation, which may have been disrupted by your abrupt stopping of the line. Even if you don't do this, the lure will generally continue to swim forward because the drag of the line in the water will straighten it out. The line acts as a stabilizing rudder. The lure will swim in the direction that the line is pointing. The more line you have in the water, the more it will act as a stabilizer.

Flippin' the Lure

Flippin' is a technique that was popularized in the late 1970s. It involves using a long rod (seven to eight feet or more) and making very short, underhand "flips" into brush and other cover. The casts are literally zero to twenty feet long, at most the length of your arms, rod, and dangling line combined. You generally don't use the reel to cast. You just "dip" your lure into brush pockets, weed pockets, and so forth. The object of this technique is to make extremely quiet casts, by laying your lure into the water instead of splashing it down as with a normal cast. A quiet approach makes a lot of sense in shallow water since fish tend to be skittish here because they have limited escape routes.

Flippin' usually occurs with heavy line, such as fifteen- to thirty-pound test. Traditionally, leadhead jigs with fiber brush guards were used with this technique.

Many flippin' fans have turned to the Flying Lure because the lures make flippin' easier and more effective. How? When using a Flying Lure to flip, you simply pitch it into places where you would normally use a jig. When the lure lands, it simply keeps on going farther under the brush or obstruction to which you have cast it. This makes the technique much more effective because you're penetrating deeper and farther into the cover than ever before. I call it flippin' plus! Flippin' fans are tuned in to the shallow-water hiding habits of bass and have an easy time understanding the Flying Lure. Even though the line size used in flippin' may exceed the recommended weights for the four-inch and six-inch Flying Lure, that's okay. Since you're generally flippin' shallow water anyway, your lure won't go any farther than a few feet underwater. In the initial stage of the lure's descent, the first few feet, a large line size will not affect the lure as much as with longer casts. You're not going for distance here, you're going for incremental penetration of the available cover. Inches make a difference.

How to Retrieve the Flying Lure

After the lure has entered the water, avoid the temptation either to start working it or to tighten the line. Let the lure sink and swim forward on its own power. As it is sinking, give it slack line. Don't be afraid to give it too much slack. You should try to keep a slight bow in the line—that is, leave the line just tight enough to form a slight arc between your rod tip and the point at which the line enters the water. This way you leave enough slack in the line to let the lure work, yet you have enough contact with the lure to know when a fish has struck. As the lure is swimming on its own, keep feeding it slack line. If you are using a spinning or a spin-casting rod, keep the bail open. As you follow the lure down with your rod tip, wait until your rod is in the horizontal position. If the lure needs more line, simply whip the rod upward in a quick motion to peel more line off your reel. This momentarily slows down your lure's forward motion, but it will speed up again immediately once you feed it more line. This shortcut allows you to strip line by using one hand only. Follow the lure down with your rod tip again and repeat this action if necessary. Another way to give the lure more line (with two hands) is simply to peel line off your reel with your left hand as you are working your rod with your right hand, or vice versa.

In working your lure with a level-wind casting reel, you can simply hold your rod steady and peel line off the reel with the hand that isn't holding the rod.

Once the first "fall," or swimming action, is complete and the lure is on the bottom, you can twitch the lure to resemble a crawfish, raise your rod tip four to six inches, and let the lure swim away in short scoots, again like a crawfish or an injured minnow.

Mostly I like to move the lure one to three feet by lifting the rod tip and then following the lure down to the bottom again. This action finds a new starting point for the lure and lets it work on its own again. Letting the lure work on its own is the key. As the lure is working, it is probing the bottom, swimming into weeds. Most important, it is maximizing the time and distance that it is falling.

HOW TO FISH THE FLYING LURE.
(Courtesy Alex Langer)

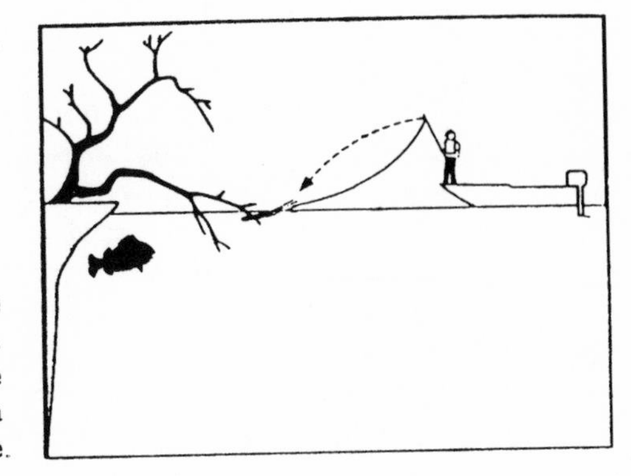

STEP 1:
Cast lure toward the area you wish to fish. When lure lands in the water, let it sink on a semi-slack line.

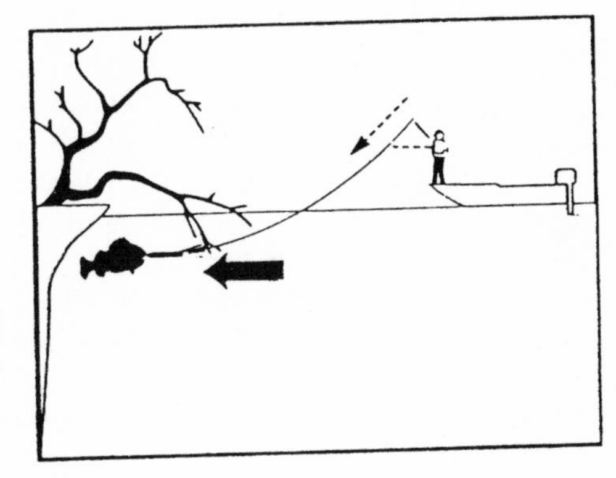

STEP 2:
Lower your rod-tip at the same rate your lure is swimming through the water, keeping a semi-slack line with a slight bow in it.

STEP 3:
When the lure has come to a stop, raise your rod tip one to three feet and repeat Step 2. Use your reel only to pick up slack line if you wish to move the lure back toward you.

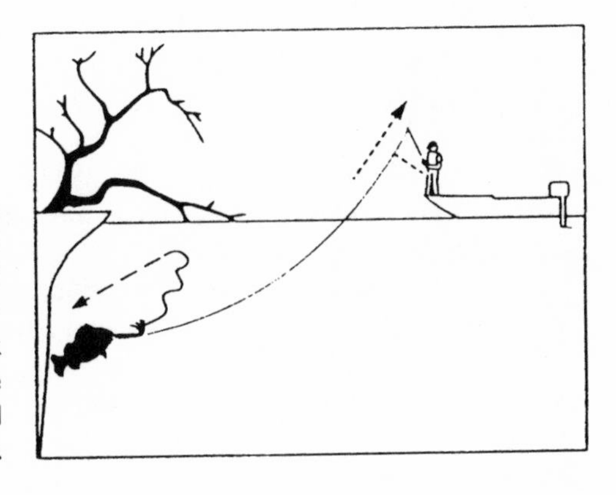

What Is the Lure Doing?

As the lure is traversing the bottom, it is important to visualize what it is doing. As you are lifting and lowering your rod tip, the lure is covering the area twice—once forward and once backward . . . once on the lift and once on the fall. It is straining the water—*twice as thoroughly as any other lure.* Fish have twice the amount of time to see it and be in contact with it . . . twice the amount of time to decide to take it. This is extremely important in neutral or negative feeding situations, when fish aren't actively chasing lures. These situations occur most of the time you are fishing. Usually fish just aren't active.

Persistence— An Introduction

Think about it this way: How much time do you spend eating during the day? One hour? Or maybe three hours at most? That's much less than 10 percent of the time during a given day. If this is true, then the reverse is also true: You're *not* eating more than 90 percent of the time. Fish eating habits vary by species and by water temperature, but you get the point. When you're not eating, you have to be enticed into eating . . . as by Aunt Bertha, when she says, "Have another cookie, just one more, oh, come on!" Even when you're not eating, you may be enticed to say "Okay, I'll have one" if the opportunity keeps presenting itself to you. Herein lies the concept of *persistence.* If a lure keeps going back to where it just came from, it has the attribute of persistence. Flying Lures, which are persistent, are like pushy salesmen!

HOW PERSISTENCE WORKS

I often enjoy fishing out of the back of someone else's boat, on his or her home lake, as a guest. Once I was fishing as a guest behind a friend whose favorite lure was a jig and pig. We fished all of his favorite places, which included docks, downed trees, and weed beds, out of a bass boat with a bow-mounted electric motor. Generally the back of the boat tends to be the worst place to fish from, since the person in the front gets first shot at all the cover. There I was, in the back. After my host took his casts at the cover, and he was a good fisherman, so did I. I proceeded to catch my first fish behind him, under a dock—about a three-and-a-half- to four-pounder. He had just skipped his jig under the dock, because it was an open one that was easy to reach underneath. It wasn't that I was reaching under cover that he couldn't reach. "How did you do that?" he asked in amazement. "Nobody catches fish behind me on this lake, especially after I've hit it with a jig and pig! How did you do it with a plastic lure?" I was smug and just smiled.

Then, at the next dock, another three-and-a-half-pound bass came to the boat caught on the Flying Lure, after my friend had already fished the dock. In this situation, catching fish after fish *behind* somebody who thinks he's a pretty good fisherman can be devastating psychologically. It's been done to me before. At this point, I had to tell him. I was, after all, his guest—and needed a ride back to shore. His lure, even though it was getting to the fish first, wasn't staying there long enough to get a bass. After the third or fourth twitch, his lure had been pulled out of the strike zone. These weren't active bass. If they were, they probably would have taken his lure when it first arrived on their doorstep. But they weren't active and his lure did not have *persistence.*

Along came my little Flying Lure, after his. It swam naturally to the bottom . . . without a hit. I lifted up my rod tip a foot or two and let it fly back under the dock. No bass again. Then I did it a third time . . . and voilà! A *strike!* That fish was convinced, or enticed, or triggered, into striking by the persistence of my lure in its face, when it wasn't actively feeding or striking conventional lures.

Fishing pro Mary Taylor once outfished a local male pro from the back of his boat in Lake Sam Rayburn in Texas. Using a Flying Lure, she outfished him eight bass to one that day because the fish had to be teased out from under the moss and wouldn't take normal plastic lures, or anything else. Mary made a believer out of him in a hurry. Nothing gets my attention as quickly as getting my hat handed to me in a given fishing situation.

Conventional lures are hit and run. That is, you work the lure past a fish. It looks at it and gets a little bit interested. You give the lure some more action (you twitch or hop a plastic worm). As you do that, you pull it away from the fish. The very action of making the lure enticing, that is, pulling on the line, moves the lure away from your quarry. I've seen it happen time and again in testing tank environments. A fish becomes interested in a lure, let's say a jig. You give it some action, the fish follows. You give it some more action and bang. You've pulled the lure just outside of that fish's range of interest. It's gone! It stops, or turns and goes back to relaxing, and you've just blown an opportunity to catch that fish forever. It happens all the time with conventional lures. There's an old saying, "You can't push a string." That's so true in fishing. With a Flying Lure, you *can* push on a string, so to speak. The action of pulling a lure back toward you is decoupled from the action of moving a lure to give it lifelike motion. In other lures, the two are one and the same. This hurts your fishing.

Next time you go to a fishing or outdoor show, look for a fish tank like the Hawg Trough and watch the demonstrations. See how many times a lure, any lure, is pulled away from the fish before it's had a chance to get interested. That's why I love to go to outdoor expos around the country with the Flying Lure. It's no contest! I win hands down—*every time!* It's just not fair. Not only do the fish respond to the preprogrammed action of the lure, but it keeps going back in their faces. It's really unfair! At the time of this writing, I have never yet failed to get at least one hit from a fish when I go up to the platform on a tank and cast into it. I often tell bystanders that if at least one bass doesn't hit a two-inch Flying Lure, they're not inactive, they're dead! Of course, in these exhibitions we bend the hooks down, so we're not actually catching the fish, we're just playing with them, like a kitten plays with a ball and yarn.

Persistence. It's opened up a whole new ball game when it comes to fishing for fish in their most common state—inactivity. Learn it and you'll outfish others, and they won't even know why. Ignore it, and you'll be missing fish you could have had.

Maximum Flying Time

The time of free fall—that is, the time between the lure's landing on the water's surface and when it lands on the bottom of the lake or ocean—is the most productive moment for any sinking lure. Fish seem to hit lures on the fall most of the time. No one has really proven why. It could have to do with the fact that the lure looks as if it's trying to escape from open water and find a hiding place on the bottom. The Flying Lure is designed to spend a maximum amount of time in free fall—the time of the cast when lures are struck the most. Its free fall really becomes a slow "swim" to the bottom, maximizing the time and the distance over which the lure falls. But the lure not only spends more time in free fall than conventional lures on the initial cast, it free falls multiple times during *each* cast. This gives the lure a much longer time to catch fish during the most productive part of the cast. Many people refer to this as getting multiple casts in one.

Less Casting Skill

Because of the Flying Lure's ability to traverse distances, you can cast short of an obstruction, yet the lure will swim right under it, better than a pro with a conventional lure could do.

Mark Stefanowicz, of Wilkes-Barre, Pennsylvania, cast the lure about three feet away from a stump and let it swim toward the stump. He writes:

> This lure was on my [six-pound test] panfish rod. At first I thought I was stuck when I felt a strong pull. The next six minutes I will never forget. As the boat got closer [to the fish], I could see that it was a large fish. I had to be careful. . . . Finally, my fishing partner was able to net the biggest bass that either of us had caught. The fish was a seven-pound four-ounce largemouth bass. . . . A lot of people laughed when I told them I sent away for your lures. Now everybody wants to borrow them. Once again, thank you very much!!!!!!
> A Flying Lure fan.

Top Water

The Flying Lure is an exceptional top-water lure. Don Meissner can fish it along the surface of the water so it looks just like a hopping frog. The hook always rides up. Just reel the lure at a slow to medium pace over the tops of weeds or lily pads, and give it a slight hopping motion with your rod tip . . . a few times per second. It's deadly! Especially when fish take a swipe at it and miss, as they often do with topwater baits, you can let the Flying Lure go retrieve them. It will swim right back in the face of a fish that just missed it. That'll usually do the trick. It's a fun way to trick fish that I taught Bass Masters Classic winner Guido Hibdon, who now regularly uses it.

What Kind of Equipment Do I Need?

In a worst-case situation, you could tie a Flying Lure onto a stick and fish it quite effectively, due to its self-propelled action. A proud grandpa once told me that he gave his three-year-old granddaughter a two-foot pole and some line . . . and she was catching fish after fish off a dock, just by working it back and forth, without a reel.

Despite this, I do recommend you get some decent equipment. A

Mark Stefanowicz and his seven-and-a-quarter-pound largemouth bass. *(Courtesy Jeff Montross)*

fairly stiff graphite, or similar lightweight, high-sensitivity rod is in order. Fiberglass is okay, but tends to be heavier and not as sensitive to fish strikes.

For most freshwater and light saltwater applications, I use a five-and-a-half to six-and-a-half-foot heavy-action spinning rod. Get a 100 percent graphite rod if you can. These are the best. The brand of reel really doesn't matter, as long as it is of good quality and matched to the rod.

You can use bait-casting equipment with the Flying Lure as well. A standard heavy-action five-and-a-half-foot jig and pig or worming outfit will do. Again, any good-quality reel is acceptable.

For saltwater, surf-casting equipment and boat rods can be used for the large saltwater-size Flying Lure. The larger nine-inch Flying Lure is made for all large saltwater species such as striped bass, tarpon, and grouper. It can also be used for large freshwater fish like musky and monster bass.

What About Line?

Use as light a line as possible—as dictated by where you are fishing.

For a two-inch Flying Lure, I recommend two- to eight-pound test line. For best results, use two- to four-pound test line. It will create less drag and will make the lure perform better.

For a four-inch Flying Lure, I recommend six- to ten-pound test line. For heavy-cover applications and flippin', twelve- through seventeen-pound test can be used.

For a six-inch Flying Lure, I recommend ten- to twelve-pound test line.

For flippin' and saltwater applications, fourteen- to twenty-plus-pound test can be used.

For a saltwater Magnum-size Flying Lure, I also recommend fourteen- to twenty-pound test and higher, depending on the application.

SPACE AGE LINES, LONG RODS

I am partial to a new generation of lines that are made of fibers such as Spectra(TM) and Kevlar(TM). These lines are much thinner and much stronger than nylon monofilament line. I have been working on a line developed just for the Flying Lure that is superthin and superstrong. This line gives the Flying Lure superb glide characteristics, very little drag, and is *super*tough. These new "miracle" fibers are the future. Spectra has already been used for some time in kite cords and for big-game fishing. Its advantage besides supertoughness? Almost no stretch! Watch for these new types of lines. Always check with the manufacturer of your rods and reels before using any of these new lines, however, because lack of stretch may damage or break some conventional rods. The new materials can damage some line guides as well. Make sure your rod and reel warranty covers the use of these new lines.

European Flying Lure fishermen use these new lines with long spinning rods of seven to nine feet. After you get used to an eight-foot spinning rod, it's really quite versatile. I'm experimenting with these long rods for use in the United States. The long rods absorb shock better, which is necessary with a line that has zero stretch, and give excellent lure and line control.

WHAT ABOUT LURE SIZE?

In general, the bigger the lure, the bigger the species of fish it will catch. But then again, there's Don Meissner's muskies and gar that he catches on two-inch lures. Go figure it out! Here are some general guidelines.

Two-inch lures catch panfish such as perch, crappie and sunfish, also spotted bass, Kentucky bass, smallmouth bass, trout, and even largemouth bass. It's a great lure for clear water and tough fishing situations. The two-inch lure will catch just about anything.

The four-inch Flying Lure is the most popular size for most freshwater species, because it most closely simulates the size of food fish in freshwater lakes. The four-inch lure is primarily used for largemouth and smallmouth bass, walleye, pike, pickerel, muskies, and large crappie. We get letters about trout and salmon being caught on the four-inch lures as well. Many people use the four-inch lure for saltwater species such as snapper, weakfish, bonefish, and stripers.

The six-inch Flying Lure is used for large freshwater fish, such as largemouth bass, walleye, musky, pike, and so forth. It's also a great top-water lure in heavy weed cover. The six-incher is the standard size for coastal saltwater fishing such as striped bass, tarpon, bonito, snook, and so forth.

The saltwater-size Flying Lure is for most saltwater species, surf casting, and monster musky fishing.

What About Color?

Color is a very local phenomenon in fishing. There are few rules and lots of exceptions.

I prefer darker colors and natural colors for clear water. These include black, pumpkinseed, and root beer Flying Lures. I also like to use Glidin' Natural Flying Lures, which are painted to resemble a variety of food fish and crawfish. If I'm fishing for largemouth bass in California, and their food fish is rainbow trout, I'll switch to a rainbow trout pattern Glidin' Natural. If smallmouth bass in Tennessee are feeding on small crawfish, I'll use a two-inch Glidin' Natural in a crawfish pattern.

For dark, muddy waters, I like to use bright colors, preferably with metalflake in them to reflect any available light. Chartreuse, electro blue, and fire and ice Flying Lures fit the bill perfectly. Pearl is also a favorite of Don Meissner's.

For waters that fall in the middle, between dark and clear, any color that works is obviously acceptable. Some of my all around favorites are tequila sunrise, red shad, and silver shad. Also, Glidin' Natural patterns that match a food species can be deadly.

Adjusting a Flying Lure

You can bend the middle of the shank of a Flying Lure jighead to give it a slight U shape when viewed from the side. This bend will give your Flying Lure a more pronounced side-to-side action. You can also impale a strand of the tail on the metal clip, in the top center of the lure, and use it as a rudder to make the lure swim left or right.

Storing Your Flying Lures

The best place to keep your Flying Lures is somewhere that keeps them perfectly flat and straight. The Flying Lure packages that they come in are perfectly designed to do that. Please don't take them out and dump them into a tackle box. If the bodies deform, they won't work correctly. Also, remember to keep colors separated. Soft vinyl plastic colors tend to "bleed" into each other if they are mixed. Take care of your tools!

Above all, experiment with your lures. Watch them work in the water. Try new approaches and new ways to fish them.

4

The Road Map to Success

Having lost sight of our objective, we redoubled our efforts.

—*Anonymous*

LANGER'S LAW #1
Fishing is simple. People make it complicated.

The Formula for Success

The objective of most people who fish is to *catch* a fish, not just to go fishing. A fish is a dull creature, a pawn of its environment—no match for a human mind. Make that most human minds. Why then do most people fail actually to catch a fish? Because they don't know how the system works. The system is *simple.* Yet most books and magazines complicate the issue by giving readers only a few pieces of the jigsaw puzzle, not the whole picture.

Despite all the books, magazines, seminars, and "magic" lures, experts have failed to make most people successful at fishing.

Most people settle for second best. They make excuses. I've heard people say, "We didn't catch anything today, but we really enjoyed the boat ride." *Wonderful*—I guess you're easily amused! Sure, it's great to be outside. Sure, it's great to be away from it all . . . but wouldn't you have more fun if you were successful at something you love?

The System Is Simple

To catch a fish, two things must happen:

1. You must *get your lure near a fish.* (Most people never get this far!) The lure must be close enough to where the fish is, so the fish knows that it's there.
2. You must *make it want to put the lure in its mouth.* (Most people don't have a clue!) The fish must actually take a piece of plastic, or some other foreign substance, and put it in its mouth. Some fishing lures seem to be designed to make fish run for cover, not munch on them. When we're fishing, we're human waiters catering to—of all things—fish!

To make these two important things happen, you must follow a very simple road map to success. In fact, the Flying Lure was designed to help the average person do exactly this: get the lure close to a fish and give the lure a self-contained action that makes the fish want to eat it. The lure is simply a tool to assist anglers on their road to fishing success.

That's why the Flying Lure has been the best-selling fishing lure in the world for the last several years—because it helps fishermen succeed.

You're about to learn the secrets of the Flying Lure Success System . . . and you don't need a Flying Lure to be successful at many aspects of it.

I developed this system over many years of fishing as well as personally interviewing and observing many of the best fishermen in the world. I developed it after speaking to thousands of people on my national radio show and in seminars around the country. It is a more thorough way to look at fishing than the traditional approaches. It will change the way you fish.

The four P's are action items for fishermen and are affected by each of the four W's. We can control each of the four P's to respond to the four W's, which we cannot control. The four P's are the "dials" by which we control the total picture. Learn to work these dials and you'll have fishing success. Each of the dials we can control are described in their own chapters (see Chapters 6, 7, 8, and 9).

THE 8 EASY STEPS TO SUCCESSFUL FISHING

THE FOUR W'S (We Can't Control)

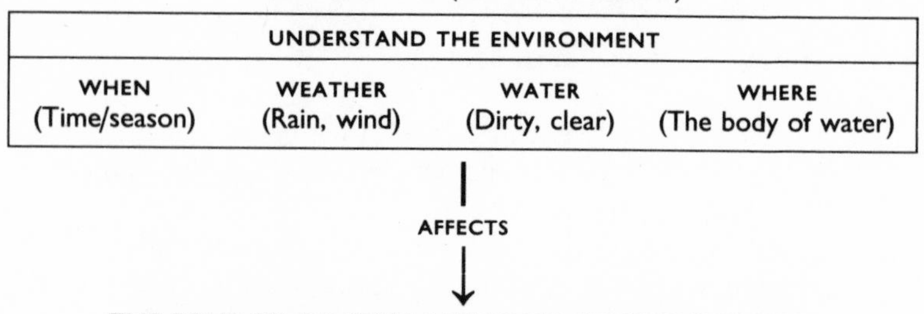

THE FOUR P'S OR "THE 4 STEPS TO FISHING SUCCESS"
(We Can Control. See chapters indicated.)

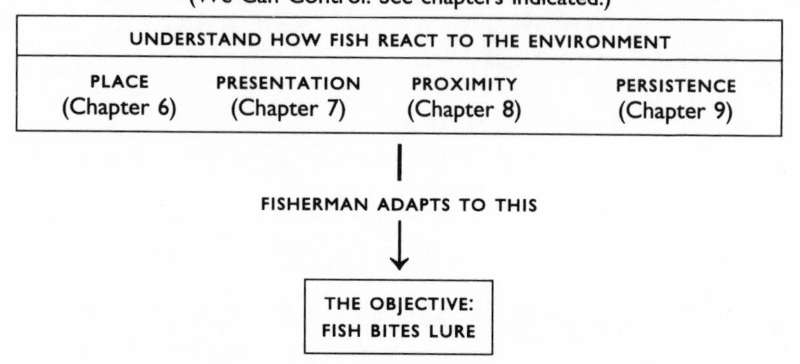

All fishing articles ever written fit somewhere into this model of fishing success. All situations you'll ever encounter can be conquered by understanding the Four Steps to Fishing Success and the thirty-three Success Questions that they are made up of. The Success Questions are a Decision Support System, to spur you toward making your own fishing decisions. It's easy! It will work for you if you give it a try.

In fishing, if you understand the *fish* and its *environment,* you've got it nailed! Honest! It's not more complicated than this. I know that it sounds too simple, but it's true.

The environment consists of four factors: the time and season, weather conditions, water conditions, and the whereabouts, or the bottom contours of the body of water you are fishing. The environment is the cause of all fish behavior—at least all fish behavior that affects us.

Alex with two big bass. *(Courtesy Alex Langer)*

The fish behave in a way that can be described by the four P's. The fish will be in a specific place and will require a specific type of lure presentation, location of the lure within a certain distance away from it (proximity), and a certain level of lure persistence.

The P's are the things we as fishermen can control. The W's are the things that are handed to us by the environment. We must respond to the W's in a way that will make us successful. And that is possible!

The following picture shows the rewards of "putting it all together" on a given day.

The Differences Between This System and Other Approaches

The Flying Lure Success System is all-inclusive. It is a checklist of items that will make you *ask the right questions* no matter where you are fishing. The system also introduces brand-new fishing concepts that beginners and pros can use to catch more and bigger fish, such as *proximity* and *persistence.* Many traditional fishing articles describe particular fishing situations, but don't necessarily give the reader a framework to translate that knowledge to other areas. For example, some traditional structure fishing articles focus on a fish's whereabouts (our place). Traditional "finesse" fishing articles that describe fishing with plastic worms focus primarily on technique (presentation). The Flying Lure Success System integrates all the important success factors in a way that anyone can understand and apply.

Asking the Right Questions Is 90 Percent of the Battle

My focus is on teaching you how to think for yourself . . . and not on a particular brand of fishing. The biggest gift you can give yourself is to teach yourself to ask the right questions. Then you can take the answers and tie them together in such a way as to give yourself action steps on the road to success.

I have developed a series of questions that will help you ask the right questions and always to seek the truth of what is happening.

THE PATH TO FISHING SUCCESS

1. →	2. →	3.
ASK EVERY POSSIBLE QUESTION TO GET EVERY POSSIBLE ANSWER THAT MATTERS Success Questions	GET THE ANSWERS FROM: • Reading articles • Knowledgeable fishermen • Experience • Observations • Local information	ASSEMBLE A GAME PLAN FOR YOUR LAKE, TIME, SPECIES, WEATHER, ETC.

Pay attention to the next fishing book or article that you read. Most likely it will tell you *what* to think, not *how* to think. Most articles and books try to tell you where, when, and how to fish in a particular way . . . and that's okay. In fact, that's necessary, but that's not what *this* book is about.

Fishermen owe a great debt to E. L. "Buck" Perry, the father of modern structure fishing. Buck was a former physics professor who first proposed the theory of structure fishing—the forerunner and basis of modern fish-finding methods. The basic tenets of structure fishing included the idea that the home of the fish is deep water and that they make periodic migrations into shallow water to feed, along defined migration routes. Buck would quarrel with the description of structure fishing as a theory. To him it was a fact. Structure fishing gained popularity in the 1950s, 1960s, and 1970s. I cut my teeth on it. *Fishing Facts* magazine, the proponent of this type of fishing, was my bible. Many writers copied Buck, adopted structure fishing as their own, built on it, and made their careers on it . . . often without thanking or acknowledging him. He was, and will always be, the Einstein of fishing.

But then, in the mid-1970s, came some studies of underwater bass behavior that contradicted pat structure fishing theories. Some studies, such as those done by underwater telemetry pioneer and biologist Mike Lembeck in lakes Miramar and El Capitan in southern California, showed that fish did not all behave in the same way. Mike followed around bass that had transmitters implanted in them and recorded their patterns of movement. Later studies in different lakes confirmed Mike's findings.

Underwater researchers discovered that there were as many as eight different behavioral groups of bass in the lakes that were studied. Some fish migrated from deep to shallow water, as structure theory suggests. Some stayed in shallow water all the time, in contradiction to the theory. Some roamed around the lake covering great distances in a single day. Some fish suspended near no cover at all (ten feet deep, over fifty feet of water), away from shore and all structure. Some huge bass were solitary loners, not school fish as previously thought. And many fish swam into the NO FISHING zones as soon as the lake was opened to fishermen just to avoid them! How is this possible? Have the fish all gone nuts? Or could they read the signs!?

Structure fishing apologists sprang into action to explain away all behaviors inconsistent with their theory. At the time, the theory was monolithic and allowed for little debate. A fish was a fish was a fish, no matter where it was, said adherents. But the apologists weren't necessary. Buck Perry had the right idea. Even Albert Einstein himself wasn't right all the time . . . but he was sure right *enough* of the time!

Take a look at nature the next time you are outside. Look at birds, dogs, and cats. Do they all behave in the same way? Of course not! For example, cats have different personalities. They respond differently to the same stimuli. Some are aggressive. Some are timid. Some are loners. Some aren't. There are more exceptions than rules. Ask a cat owner. Can it be said that all cats will generally act in the same way given a set of conditions? Maybe. Maybe not. Underwater photography pioneer Glen Lau has done extensive research on what traits make a bass a large "superbass." A superbass has different behavioral and feeding characteristics from a lesser "normal" bass. Do you see my point?

If fish were a monolithic community, all tournaments would be won or lost on the same fishing pattern. On any given lake on any given day, there are a number of patterns on which fish are caught: shallow, deep, and God knows where—on lots of different lures!

Fish are different. Believe it! We can make some generalizations based on the work of Buck Perry and others. However, there are nuances of behavior that make a South Carolina bass in Lake Murray different from a Missouri bass in Truman Lake. Not much different, but sometimes just enough! Ask the pros who fish the national circuits. They'll tell you it's so. It took me a long time to discover this, as an early adherent of the structure theory. Much of fishing is by the seat of your pants—that is, discovering things about a lake as you go along. Some of your original discoveries can and will be the key to fishing a particular body of water on a given day.

Bill Plummer—One of the Quiet Founders of Modern Fishing

Bill Plummer has probably caught more bass than anyone in history. That is not hyperbole; I believe it is a statement of pure fact. He has caught thousands of bass each year, including an inordinate number of monsters from northern lakes. From ice-out to ice-in, Bill fishes five to seven days per week and has done so for over thirty years. At 2,000 bass per year, which is one of the estimates, that's over 60,000 bass! He started fishing for bass before modern bass fishing was invented. And he certainly helped popularize it. He has been written up by every major magazine in the industry and is the inventor of the first soft top-water artificial frog, the Bill Plummer Frog.

Bill fishes the simple way—from a wooden boat that he has designed, with oars, no electric motor, no sonar, no bells and whistles, just a small gas motor on the back. He has learned the habits of bass by trial and error and deduction, not by book learning. There were no books to learn from when he first started. He is a solitary hunter, who learns and learns and learns. Bill exemplifies the ideals that we should have as fishermen: a respect for the fish . . . and a constantly open mind that learns yet is not prone to gimmickry or rigid theories. I have learned a lot from Bill and am proud to call him my friend. Strive always to learn and be flexible. Strive to be analytical like Buck Perry, and adaptable like Bill Plummer.

Sometimes There Are More Exceptions Than Rules

Some lakes behave opposite of what you would expect. Bright, sunny cold-front days were great on Lake Cochituate, in Natick, Massachusetts, in the summertime. These days should have been tough and unproductive. Cloudy days were bad. They should have been good for fishing. I won a tournament on this lake when I was eighteen years old and beat more seasoned competitors from a number of states because I figured out how it worked. I spent months on that lake practicing until I knew exactly how the bass there responded to all types of situations. No book on fishing had these answers.

You Need to Build a Model

You need to build a model in your mind as to how a particular body of water works. For example, "If it's sunny, fish will generally be here and take this size and color of lure. If it's cloudy, fish will be shallower and take another type of lure presentation." You've got to *visualize* it in your mind. You've got to almost feel what the fish feel and how they react to the environment. This kind of knowledge for a specific body of water is not found in books or magazines. The one danger of adhering to any theory of fishing, no matter how worthwhile, is that you tend to interpret all data in light of that theory and you may be blinded to obvious facts that don't fit in. Read all the books and articles that you can, but blend the information in with your own experience and above all, experiment.

Bill Plummer, with a huge bass caught in the 1960s! *(Courtesy Norma Plummer)*

Don't Beat Yourself Up!

In the past I've made the mistake of applying a specific article that I had read to a specific lake I was fishing, and went away thinking that there was something wrong with me. What was wrong was that the fish in my lake weren't responding at all like the fish in the article. I was trying to cram the reality of my lake into the article's framework. It doesn't work. You can get general knowledge from literature; then you must go out and make your own discoveries. I wish more writers would admit that to themselves and to their readers. You can't neatly decree a truth in fishing and expect it to be so, everywhere, all the time, even in similar situations.

To find reality, to be a seeker of truth, in fishing, you have to ask questions all the time and learn all the time. I have developed a set of simple questions called the Fishing Success Questions. You will find them explained in Chapters 5 through 9. If you answer them correctly, they can give you fishing success.

The thirty-three Success Questions force you to think about how the environment, or the uncontrollable factors thrust upon us by nature (the 4 W's), affect the 4 P's (the factors we can control). If we understand how to take command of the factors we *can* control, and not worry about those that we can't, we can become successful at any type of fishing we choose.

5

Your Crash Course in Fishing

Introduction to the Fishing Success Questions

Everything You Ever Wanted to Know About Fishing But Didn't Know to Ask

If someone were to walk up to you and say "I can teach you to fish in four steps" or "You're just thirty-three questions away from fishing success. Answer these questions correctly, and you'll be successful," you'd listen, wouldn't you? Well, that's exactly what I'm saying to you right now.

The Decision Support System (thirty-three Fishing Success Questions) that I'm about to share with you is a checklist I've compiled over many years. Even more, it is a system to help you get to the facts that will help you catch more and bigger fish—anywhere you are, whatever you're fishing for. How is this possible? you might ask. All the books and magazines you might read give you answers and not questions. Yes, the answers are important, and I encourage you to get and read every intelligent article you can. You will need answers. But the questions or the framework is even more important because it will tell you what information you *should* be looking for. And if the book or article you're reading or expert whom you're talking to doesn't have it, you'll know to ask for it and get it!

I am about to make a confession. I know nothing about fishing in the Desna River in Novogorod Seversk in the Ukraine, in Russia. It is the river where my grandmother, an avid fisherwoman, spent her early years in the late 1800s fishing. She was a fanatical fisherwoman, fishing long days and nights on that river with great success. As hooks, she used bent over sewing needles—the same kind she made for me when I was a kid. It was she who first taught me to fish. Assuming I were to go to that river in Russia today, knowing nothing about its fish, weather, and water conditions, or anything else, how would I ever catch fish?

I might be helped a little bit by reading articles about fishing in the United States . . . but give me the thirty-three Universal Fishing Success Questions and a few days, and I promise you I would start catching fish. Why? Because all fish are affected by the same environmental forces: the season *(when),* the *weather, water* conditions, and the fish's *where*abouts.

These four environmental factors affect the four activities that we as fishermen control: the *place* where we are fishing, the *presentation* of the lure, the *proximity* of the lure to the fish, and the *persistence* of our lure. If we understand how the 4 W's affect the 4 P's and what we can do, we have the tools to conquer any fishing situation. Now, that's confidence!

So whether you're fishing for smallmouth bass in Tennessee or giant catfish in the Amazon River, you have the mental tools to succeed.

This approach welcomes any and all new information, and is not threatened by new knowledge, as many other fishing theories are. New knowledge is sought and encouraged. Also, this system seeks out and incorporates local factors, which many publications often overlook.

James Beasley of Midway, Georgia, wrote to tell me that he has begun to keep a log of the fish he catches. Now, there's a guy who can succeed! Keeping a log of all the new information and fishing experiences that you are having with this system is a way to supercharge your learning. He sent us a photo of a six-and-three-quarter-pound bass caught on the Flying Lure. He's off to a great start! I remember some structure fishing adherents in the 1970s who didn't feel right unless they were fishing deep-water areas such as dropoffs. At the time many articles about structure stressed fishing deep-water structure. I heard a number of them say so! Many failed at fishing tournaments that I was running at the time because they blindly followed a system. Don't do this! Don't be intellectually lazy. Always question what is happening. Even question

James Beasley of Georgia with a nice bass. *(Courtesy Betty Beasley)*

my questions, and add your own if you like! If you're not catching fish, go back and review the questions to spur your own thinking. Succeed—it's in your power.

How the System Works

All we're trying to do is to see, one step at a time, how nature's uncontrollable forces (the 4 W's) affect our controllable responses (the 4 P's). Let's take a look at Chapter 6. Answering the questions in Chapter 6 will help us determine the *place* where we should be fishing.

The following table explains what chapter provides the answers to what questions. Looking closer at Chapter 6, Questions 3 through 5, help us answer how the *place* we are fishing is determined by *when* we are fishing. Questions 6 through 10 tell us how *weather* affects the place we are fishing, and so forth.

Chapter 7 gives us a path to determine the kind of lure *presentation* we should have.

Chapter 8 tells us how to arrive at the *proximity* that a lure needs (to be near the fish).

Chapter 9 tells us the *persistence* with which we should be fishing on a given day.

When you have gone through all the questions, you will know how each of nature's forces (when, weather, water, and where) determine what we should be doing (place, presentation, proximity, and persistence).

You are now armed with the keys to master any fishing situation. Only you will provide the answers.

THE DECISION SUPPORT SYSTEM: FOUR STEPS TO SUCCESS

Questions 1 and 2, the superquestions, are discussed later in this chapter. These two questions deal with the big picture only.

THE 4 P'S	THE FOUR W'S NATURE CONTROLS			
WE CONTROL	WHEN	WEATHER	WATER	WHERE
PLACE⟶ (Chapter 6)	Questions: 3,4,5	Questions: 6,7,8,9,10	Questions: 11,12,13 14,15	Questions: 16,17,18,19
PRESENTATION⟶ (Chapter 7)	Questions: 20,21,22	Question 23	Question 24	Question 25
PROXIMITY⟶ (Chapter 8)	Question 26	Question 27	Question 28	Question 29
PERSISTENCE⟶ (Chapter 9)	Question 30	Question 31	Question 32	Question 33

The Ultimate Magazine and Book Test

Armed with the thirty-three Fishing Success Questions, you can now dissect any book or magazine article and get what you need. You'll know if the article is answering only Questions 1 through 5 and ignoring the rest. You'll know if it applies only to some waters and not necessarily to yours. You'll be able to modify methods to fit the lake you are fishing. You'll be able to get the answers to the rest of the questions, or at least know where the holes in the information are. You're no longer at the mercy of others. By the way, if any article answers even half of the thirty-three questions, it's probably a pretty good one!

Beginning Your Quest

Before you even begin looking for fish, you must acknowledge what you're fishing for and what time of year it is. Simple? You bet. Believe it or not, most people never get that far.

If you don't know what fish you're looking for, how are you ever going to find it?

What Species Do the Questions and Answers Refer To?

I have tried to keep the answers to the questions general guidelines to spur your own thinking rather than giving you pat answers. Where the species of fish isn't indicated, I am referring to freshwater North American warm-water fish in general and largemouth bass in particular. Other species are referred to sometimes as well. Good luck!

The Superquestions

"Superquestions" refers to questions 1 and 2 only. They are a synopsis of the thirty-three success questions.

QUESTION 1. WHAT SPECIES OF FISH AM I FISHING FOR?

You have to decide. Most people never do. Fishing for "anything" doesn't cut it. Know who your customer is . . . and . . . know what your customer wants.

Young Alex with a nine-and-a-quarter-pound bass. *(Courtesy Alex Langer)*

Sometimes I ask people fishing from shore "What are you fishing for?" They reply, "I dunno!" I'll guarantee you, the only thing you'll consistently catch with that attitude is a cold. And it's too bad. An old saying says: A journey of a thousand miles begins with a single step. In fishing, that first step is to determine what fish exist wherever you are fishing and then to decide what fish you are going after.

Where I grew up, a largemouth bass was my game fish of choice. I followed, learned about, and admired those green, potbellied ghosts. They became almost mystical creatures to me. But I had to make the decision to be a bass fisherman first. Other fishermen in the same lakes that I fished became trout fishermen. Trout were the recognized "true" game fish in my neighborhood. At times, I learned about, followed, and caught trout as well. But it was not by accident. In the same lakes, bass and trout were found in different places, took different lures, and required a different set of skills to catch.

Focus all of your skills on one fish first, whatever it may be. Learn, study, and get to know everything about its habits, likes, and dislikes. Once you learn the "language" of one fish, the next one will be easier since many of the same skills apply.

Decide and focus!

QUESTION 2. WHAT TIME OF THE YEAR IS IT?

Fish behave differently as the calendar changes. Actually, they don't believe in our calendars—they go by the earth's calendar. The fish calendar is mostly dependent on water temperature, although not entirely so. As you seek one species of fish, you need to know about those changes that occur in fish behavior as the calendar changes. More about this later.

See? So far fishing is simple!

6

Place—
Where Are the Fish?

LANGER'S LAW #2
Fish are always somewhere.

These questions will help you determine the *place* you should be fishing given a certain time of year, in different types of weather and water conditions, and on different bodies of water.

QUESTION 3. WHERE SHOULD I BE FISHING AT THIS TIME OF THE YEAR?

CHECKLIST
- Shallow
- Medium
- Deep
- Roaming
- Spawning
- Suspending

Once you determine the species of fish you're after and the time of year, you need to learn about the species' behavior at this time. Fish are at the mercy of the forces that control them—not unlike some people I know. They cannot pick up, put all their belongings in a FISH U-HAUL, and move to another lake. They're stuck. They must use whatever cover is available to them to do whatever their biological instincts tell them to do at this time of year.

You must determine, in general, how fish behave in the spring, summer, fall, and winter. This information is easily obtainable from books and magazines. In fact, this is where many books and magazines stop. After telling you about fish behavior in general, they let you go on to apply it to your own body of water.

Most fish in North America that are considered warm-water species, such as bass, pike, and panfish, tend to spawn in the spring, in shallower water. Then in the summertime their location generally is based on deeper cover and protection from other large fish. Summer behavior patterns tend to be food-oriented. That is, the metabolism of fish is higher then than at other times and they are feeding more frequently. Therefore, food is a primary consideration. Find the food and the cover, and you'll usually find the fish.

In the fall the same warm-water fish will move shallower to gorge themselves on food before winter.

In the winter fish become less active because their metabolism slows as the water cools. Therefore, they feed much less frequently. They swim into deeper, more stable water. That's why it's tougher to catch fish as the water becomes colder and it's easier as the water becomes warmer.

In the spring, as the water warms, the location of fish relates to spawning. They tend to feed heavily before the spawn and very little during and after it. Their biological needs dictate where they will be at this time of year. As the water warms, these fish revert to summer patterns . . . and so it goes, over and over as the years go by.

The key is to find out how *your* fish of choice responds to seasonal changes. If your species of fish is a warm-water fish, such as a bass, I have just given you some quick guidelines. It is impossible to cover all species in this book, so pick the fish you're after and start answering the questions!

QUESTION 4. WHERE DO THE FISH SPEND MOST OF THEIR TIME? WHERE DO THEY LIVE? WHAT TIME DO THEY FEED?

During this time of the year, where does the fish you're seeking call home? As we learned in the last chapter, bass were once believed to live in deep water in the summer and to migrate shallower when they fed. We found out that actually there were a number of groups of bass that behaved differently. Some lived shallow, some deep. Written information is probably available for any fish you are seeking. Find it in libraries, or better yet, go to some tackle shops and ask the local experts. They'll get you on the road quickly because it's in their interest that you succeed. They may not have the full picture, but you can begin filling in the answers to the thirty-three questions from all available sources.

Keep records every time you go fishing. Trial and error is the most valuable source of information you will find in fishing. I believe it is one of the immutable laws of the universe. Integrate this knowledge with your "book" knowledge.

What Time Are They Feeding?

You can predict the exact time that fish feed on a given day if you fish a body of water enough. If you are fishing salt water, the times are much more predictable than fresh water. In saltwater fishing, the feeding times are usually on a rising or on a falling tide . . . but not always. In fresh water, the best times tend to be dawn and dusk . . . but not always. Some of the best fishing times I've experienced have been with the afternoon sun blazing—2 to 4 P.M.! Why? I'm not sure. In different bodies of water, fish follow different cycles. Even adjacent lakes can be very different in fish behavior and timing. The message here is, fish do have preferred feeding times on different bodies of water. These times are best determined by trial and error, by fishing the waters week in and week out. In my opinion, there's no other way.

Often in a tournament, most anglers have the same story: "The fish all turned on at 8 A.M. and turned off at 9:30 A.M. . . . we didn't get any steady action for the rest of the day." Why does this happen? No one really knows. Be an observer of nature, and use your observations to your advantage.

What About Solar and Lunar Periods?

I honestly don't know! I'm not sure that anybody does, or can prove it. Lunar periods are the time when the moon's gravitational pull is the strongest on the earth in a particular place. To put it another way, if everybody had an ocean across the United States (I've heard that somewhere before), it would be high tide there during the lunar period because that is when the moon's gravitational pull on the earth and water is at its strongest. When is it high tide in Peoria? When there's a lunar period, of course! Fishing is supposed to be the best during these periods. Is it really? Some people say so. I have even heard of claims that most big fish caught in outdoor magazine contests held for the past fifty or so years have been caught primarily during these periods.

I am never one to pooh-pooh an idea if I can't prove it to be either true or false. Perhaps there are times when the pull of the moon has an effect on fish. It's possible. There is anecdotal evidence of large fish being caught when a moon phase occurs just as the leading edge of a weather front passes over an area. Would these same fish have been caught due to the effects of the weather system alone? There is no proof.

A few interactions between the moon and fish can be proven. Often spawns of various types of fish occur around a specific phase of the moon. That's one of the handful of concrete proofs we have in a very specific situation.

Until there is conclusive proof one way or another, I never let lunar periods dictate when I am fishing. I go fishing whenever I can.

You can get all kinds of information from books and magazines, but be careful! Local conditions may change the data a great deal. We'll get to this when we discuss the effects of *where* the fish are in questions 16 through 19.

QUESTION 5. AT THIS TIME OF YEAR, WHERE DOES YOUR QUARRY FEED?

CHECKLIST

- Depth
- Weeds
- Cover
- Other characteristics

Where fish live is often different from where fish feed at a given time of year. Fish often live in deeper water and then come shallower to feed on a food shelf, which is generally a fertile, weed-filled area. Food shelves often contain plankton that minnows, crayfish, and other food species feed on. The presence of the food species draws the game fish we are after to the area.

For example, in Port Charlotte harbor, Florida, on the Gulf of Mexico, redfish often live in deeper channels when they are not feeding. When they begin to feed, they move into grassy shallow sandbars and under mangrove trees. Some redfish, however, never leave the mangrove roots.

So, it's important to know where fish live *and* where they feed. If they're not feeding, you want to know where they are, so you can tease them into striking with a lure that has *persistence.*

The "Weather" Questions

These questions will help you answer how weather conditions affect where fish generally will be (place).

If you have answered the when questions (3 through 5), you should know where the fish you are seeking lives, where it feeds, whether it is in deep water or shallow, and other basic facts about the place you should be fishing. Now, by answering the weather questions, you will see how weather will affect the place you should be fishing.

QUESTION 6. WHAT IS THE LIGHT PENETRATION AND HOW DOES IT AFFECT LOCATION?

Sunlight that enters the water affects many fish species negatively. In general, most fish do not like light. Light makes them feel exposed and vulnerable. They prefer to see but not be seen. Therefore, no matter what time of the year it is, the level of light penetrating the water will affect the location of most fish.

Quite simply, a bright day tends to make fish concentrate more around objects or obstructions, near shade. Cloudy days tend to allow fish to disperse more, no matter what time of the year it is.

So, what is the practical application of light penetration? In general, the following holds true.

UNDER CLOUDY CONDITIONS:

- If fish are deep, they will tend to move shallower.
- If fish are concentrated under cover, they will tend to roam and scatter more than before.
- If fish were inactive in shallow water, they will tend to become more active.

UNDER SUNNY CONDITIONS:

- If fish were shallow, they will tend to move deeper.
- If fish are scattered, they will tend to concentrate near shade-producing cover and weeds.
- If fish were active in shallow water, they will tend to become less active.

Please note, these are generalities only! Some fish are not light-averse. Also, when fish are spawning, their biological duties take over, and they tolerate light. Also note that *changes* in light conditions are much more significant than the absolute level of light. Changes tend to disorient fish.

The photograph shows Don Meissner and Ray Lentine fishing under cloudy conditions. The bass were dispersed that day and hitting both conventional spinnerbaits and Flying Lure spinnerbaits. Don borrowed my large rain suit that day . . . can you tell?

In a testing tank, when the lights are unexpectedly dimmed, fish instantly turn off and will remain inactive for at least fifteen to thirty minutes. Theoretically, a lower level of light should turn *on* the fish. Not so.

So, no matter where a fish is during the course of the year, the level of light will have an effect on its location.

Study your quarry to find out the degree to which light affects it.

QUESTION 7. HOW DO COLD FRONTS AFFECT LOCATION AND FEEDING?

CHECKLIST

- Reduce or increase feeding?
- Concentrate fish under obstructions?
- Make fish go deeper?
- No effect?

Everybody knows what cold fronts are. They're those jaggy lines on Willard's weather map that blow across an area and change the temperature from warmer to cooler. In the summer months, cold fronts generally get rid of the muggy weather and bring in delightful sunny skies. Delightful for everyone but fishermen! A cold front can bring with it turbulent weather and electrical storms because of the violent clash between warm and cold air masses. But cold fronts also bring with them bright sunny skies and perhaps some other changes that we don't fully understand—that often turn off fishing. After a cold front, it's as if somebody pushed a "reset" button on the lake. Fish are often shut off and set the snooze alarm for a day, or two, or three. Some species are more affected than others. Largemouth bass tend to take cold fronts much more personally than smallmouth bass. Smallmouth tend to be a lot more active after a cold front than their green cousins.

Don Meissner and Ray Lentine fishing in the rain. *(Courtesy Jim Caldwell)*

I believe that increased light penetration is only a part of the answer to why cold fronts generally put a damper on fishing. Other factors must be at play, such as a sudden temperature and pressure change . . . and probably other things as well that we have not yet identified.

In fishing, many writers and thinkers tend to be very sure about what they think they know and ignore what they don't know. If we don't have a full grasp of the effects of certain factors, such as why cold fronts are bad, we should admit it. I do.

So then, how do cold fronts affect location?

- They concentrate fish under and near obstructions.
- They make some fish go deeper. Even if fish are on the spawning beds, they will make some fish move off. A number of people called me on my radio show to report just such a condition that was occurring in the spring of 1993 in Florida. As soon as the fish were ready to spawn, they were driven off repeatedly by a series of cold fronts, making what was already a late spring even later. If cold fronts were an issue of light penetration alone, the strong biological urge of bass to spawn would not have been interrupted, since non–cold front days can offer similar light conditions with no negative consequences.
- They usually make most fish inactive or less active.

There are some species on which cold fronts seem to have little effect, especially in the ocean. One of my favorite lakes even has an oddball condition, where a cold front brings out the bass in droves and turns them on. It's the exceptions that make fishing fun, not the rules!

QUESTION 8. STABILITY INDEX: HAS THE WEATHER AND WATER BEEN STABLE? FOR HOW MANY DAYS? HOW DOES A LACK OF STABILITY AFFECT THE SPECIES?

CHECKLIST OF VARIABLES.

- Air temperature
- Air pressure
- Wind direction
- Light penetration
- Precipitation
- Relative humidity
- Water currents
- Water level
- Other key factors (e.g., power plant emissions)

Stability in weather conditions is the single best predictor of fishing success on a given day. That's an important statement. Read it again. More than anything, fish crave a stable environment. Changes in the weather make fish move, change location, and adjust to uncertain circumstances.

Stable weather entrenches fish in their locations and feeding patterns. If they are predators, stable weather seems to make them happier and better and more confident in what they do.

One of the best bass fishing days I ever had, where I caught big fish after big fish, on two different lakes, occurred at the end of an almost two-week–long period of stability. It was an endless summer. For all of this time, the weather was hot, sunny, and muggy. No fronts passed through the area. The light penetration was high, but stable, as was the humidity, temperature, and pressure. The fish seemed to be active all day, jumping on just about anything I would throw. With one or two exceptions, every bass was five to six pounds or better.

Stability does not move fish. It makes fish much more aggressive wherever they are.

Although stability is so important a measure, nobody has ever quantified it. I am currently refining a working framework for an index for stability. Until we can quantify the concept of stability, you must be a weather watcher. Keep a thermometer and a barometer handy, and watch TV weather reports.

Keep track of the key weather variables in your area. Every day that the temperature stays within five degrees of the day before, the barometric pressure stays stable, the wind direction does not change drastically, and precipitation and light penetration are about the same as the day before, you have stability.

For every day that comes with no major changes from the day before, I score 1 point. So every point means one day of stability. A point is just a way I use to keep score when I'm tracking the weather. As the points keep adding up, I know the fishing is getting better. When I count up to 7 points or more I make sure I go to my favorite lake if I can—as soon as possible.

ALEX'S WEATHER STABILITY INDEX

Temperature	5 degrees plus or minus
Pressure	Same

Wind direction	From the same direction(s) as the day before (within a quadrant)
Light penetration	Same general light situation as day before
Precipitation	Same as day before

In the following table, the points of stability, are general guidelines. In some areas of the Midwest, weather patterns seldom give more than a few days (or hours) of stability. In other areas, weeks of stable weather are common. On the whole, fishing is better in stable climates. In general, if there have been at least two to four days of stability in a given area, there is an excellent chance that fish are feeding well and established in their patterns. If you have a week or more of stable weather, fishing could get exciting!

POINTS OF STABILITY		FISHING OUTLOOK
0–1 day of stability	=	poor
1–2 days of stability	=	fair
2–3 days of stability	=	good
3–5 days of stability	=	excellent
5–7 days of stability	=	exceptional
7 + days of stability	=	hold on!

Other factors in the overall stability index are the water levels in the lake or river and any other variable that affects the environment's stability. For example, you may have all the stable weather you want, and the local residents' association decides to put a weed killer in the water. The water changes from clear to murky. Your stability has just been blown!

Once any of the major factors in the stability index change, you should push the "reset" button and start counting from zero again. Study the weather and keep notes about how it affects your fishing.

The two boys in the picture that follows caught a mess of flounder off a pier in South Boston. This flounder "bite" was brought on by a week of sunny, stable May weather back in the early 1970s. Do you recognize the kid on the left?

QUESTION 9. HOW DOES PRECIPITATION AFFECT LOCATION?

CHECKLIST

- Has rain made the water cloudy?
- Did snow/rain cool or warm the surface temperature of the water?
- Are there contaminants in the rain? Is the pH or oxygen content affected?

Precipitation affects the location of fish in a very direct way. Rain can either cool or warm the surface water in a lake or ocean. If the rain cools

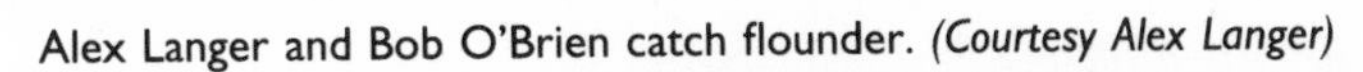

Alex Langer and Bob O'Brien catch flounder. *(Courtesy Alex Langer)*

the water, a number of species may move into deeper water or may become less active. Rain warming the water in the fall can have a positive effect on feeding. Always compare the water's surface temperature with the air temperature. If the surface temperature of the water changes more than one to two degrees Fahrenheit, the precipitation will often spur location changes in fish in shallow water.

Rain's most important attribute usually is that it discolors a body of water. Discoloration occurs because the rain causes earth to wash into the water from shore and from incoming rivers and streams. Discoloration often makes fish more prone to roam away from cover, since it decreases light penetration and makes them more scattered.

If fish are used to clear water and a heavy rain discolors it significantly, fish that rely on their good eyesight can become much tougher to catch. This situation occurred in California in the spring of 1993, when there were unusually strong rains. Largemouth bass, which were used to crystal-clear water, became much more difficult to catch. Dirty water threw them for a loop. On the other hand, fish that are used to muddy reservoirs don't care a bit if the water gets cloudy. It can actually turn them on and bring them closer to shore.

Acid rain has been a great problem in some parts of the United States. Airborne contaminants that are deposited in lakes by rainfall increase the acidity of a lake, actually killing off some species of fish, such as trout. The effects of acid rain are especially strong in small lakes, where water often takes on a tea-colored, tannic look. Some fish will actually have yellowish instead of white bellies. Fish locations may become slightly shallower due to the water coloration.

Always be aware of precipitation. It can change fishing instantly.

QUESTION 10. HAVE THERE BEEN ANY ABNORMAL WEATHER CONDITIONS? ARE SOME COMING? HOW WILL THIS AFFECT WHERE FISH WILL BE?

When a weather front is about to pass through where I'm fishing, I'm excited about the possibilities of catching big fish. Again, no one knows exactly why weather fronts are positive events for fish, but they seem to be. The same cold fronts that bring bad fishing conditions and clear skies *after* they blow through can bring some tremendous fishing *just before* they move through.

I have caught many big bass just before the high winds and thunder started. One experience in particular I will always remember, because I believe that I came very close to being killed. I was fishing on Whitehall Reservoir in central Massachusetts, shortly after I had invented the Flying Lure on the same lake. This lake is famous for its overhanging brush and floating islands that hold big bass.

A front had just begun to blow through. As it did so, I could see the clouds and feel the air mass becoming colder and drier. Foolishly, I did not get off the lake fast enough, because the fishing was exceptional. The fish were goofy! I literally caught eight fish on eight casts. I saw the lightning in the distance. The fish were jumping on my line—big ones and little ones—just seconds before the thunder started. At the last second, I beached my boat on the nearest point and started praying. Torrential rains filled my boat with a hundred gallons of water in minutes. The rain was so heavy that I feared I couldn't breathe! I saw lightning hit the dam at the end of the lake. Then I saw the lightning come closer and hit the point between me and the dam. It was an awful explosion. I was on the next point. Then the woods exploded behind me! The lightning had hit the point I was beached on. The ground shook. I was afraid to breathe. The sky was so black, it looked as if someone had hung a concrete slab above me. Minutes went by and the rain kept falling. Then it began to lighten up. In about ten minutes, the front had passed over me. I couldn't believe I was still alive.

Please don't ever do what I did. I was a nineteen-year-old kid at the time. It was stupid! No fish is worth dying for—and I came very close. When you're on the water in a lightning storm, you're the highest point on the water and have a great chance of being hit. If you see or hear that lightning may be coming, get off the water.

If you observe a front moving past you a few times, even from your car, you'll be amazed at how predictable they are. First clouds, then a rush of air, then it gets colder, the wind keeps blowing, then torrential rain and thunder . . . then cooler, drier air . . . and it's over. Once when a friend and I were out on the water, we were caught in a front with no time to make it back to the boat ramp. I told him to watch what was happening as I called it out, step by step. We observed the front from under a bridge where we beached the boat. After the front pulled away, in about fifteen minutes, he looked at me in amazement and said, "How did you do that?" as if I controlled the elements. "Observation, my dear Watson," I said. "Observation."

I advise fishing fronts as they move through, but from a safe distance—hours, not minutes, before they pass.

But I have a theory. I asked a physicist friend of mine about it once.

He replied that the polarity of the earth's charge changes when a thunderstorm approaches. One company makes a device that measures the charge of the earth and warns boaters and golfers when it changes prior to a thunderstorm. Eureka! I thought. This is it! The unseen factor that leads a storm front could be the change in the earth's electrical charge. I believe this is the secret variable, or at least one of them. Perhaps this change in the earth's electrical charge affects the electrical systems of fish in some way to make them aggressive.

The "Water" Questions

The following questions help you answer how water conditions affect where fish generally will be.

QUESTION 11. HOW DOES WATER COLOR AFFECT LOCATION?

CHECKLIST.
IN GENERAL,
– Colored water = Shallower fish
– Clear water = Deeper fish

The rule of thumb in fishing as it pertains to water color is that darker, dirtier water reduces the amount of sunlight entering the water. Consequently, most fish species tend to move shallower than in a similar lake with clear water.

In any given season, a clearing of the water will tend to make fish go deeper or will make them much more prone to hide from the sunlight under visible cover or weeds.

Water color usually becomes darker if:

- Rain washes earth or debris into the water.
- Organic matter such as fallen trees and weeds decompose. Dirty-looking water is not necessarily polluted water.
- Currents in a reservoir wash up the earth or clay bottom.
- Pollution or acid rain enters the water.
- A lake "turns over" in the fall. Turnover occurs when the surface water turns 39° F. At this temperature, water is at its densest and sinks to the bottom. The water at the bottom of the lake boils up and emits suspended particles of decaying weeds and leaves into the water. This can be a poor time to fish because suspended particles keep fish inactive.

In the fall of 1992 Guido Hibdon, Dion Hibdon, and I went fishing in Oneida Lake in upstate New York, right after the lake turned over. The suspended particles in the water were so pervasive that we caught (actually, Guido did!) only one bass all morning. Guido believes that bass don't want to tangle this debris in their gills and therefore become inactive until the turnover passes. We went to another, clear body of water later the same day and mopped up.

QUESTION 12. HOW DOES THE WATER TEMPERATURE AFFECT LOCATION?

Water temperature affects the location of fish primarily by its changing through the seasons. A certain temperature will cause fish to spawn in the spring, move into a summer feeding pattern, or reduce their activity in the winter. Bass will start to spawn in the 62° to 64° F. range and will tend to move off the spawn in the 68° range.

During a fish's spawning period, changes in water temperature can throw it off its spawn, interrupting the process.

Many fish do have a preferred operating range. In the past, so-called preferred temperature ranges were supposed to tell us where certain fish species would be. Largemouth bass were said to have a preferred temperature of 72° F. The implication was, find the temperature and you'll find the fish. Unfortunately, it's not that easy! Bass operate in all temperature ranges. However, once the temperature gets far above or below the operating range, fish will tend to slow down. Fish react as we humans do. We like it at 72°, but once the temperature hits 85°, some of us don't move as quickly as before.

My three guidelines for temperature as it affects *place* are:

1. Water temperature affects a fish's seasonal cycles. Follow the cycles and best places by following the water temperature in a body of water.
2. Any sudden changes in water temperature are a shock to a fish's system and will affect fishing negatively.
3. Water temperature affects the speed with which a fish's metabolism operates. The higher the metabolism, the more the fish's location will depend on following the available food in a given body of water.

QUESTION 13. DOES PH AFFECT LOCATION?

CHECKLIST

- Look for the preferred pH zone of a fish.
- Find the tolerance of a fish to different pH levels.

pH meters that test the alkalinity versus acidity of water have long been available to the fishing public. It's like testing the water in your goldfish bowl at home. Still, pH meters are esoteric items not used by the masses. I believe that under some situations, finding the right pH level for the species you're looking for can make the difference between fish and no fish.

I do not personally own a pH meter at the moment, although I know of people who swear by them. I think a pH meter is a tool in your arsenal that you might consider as you get more experienced in the sport and have some money to spend.

QUESTION 14. ARE THERE WATER CURRENTS THAT AFFECT THE LOCATION OF FISH?

CHECKLIST

- Look for currents or tides that sweep food by any particular places, such as jetties, docks, riprap, and the like. Predators can lie in wait here.
- Look for any dead spots, pools, or eddies *near* an area where current flows by quickly.
- The presence of current may make a spot that would otherwise hold fish unusable.
- Raising or lowering the water level in a reservoir creates edges between moving water and quiet water.

When I was in my teens, I thought I knew how to fish every kind of water . . . until I fished a river. The same places that would surely have held a fish didn't have one within miles! Why? Because current is often the fourth dimension in seeking a *place* to fish. Trees where the current created quiet places for predators to hide were the trees that held fish—trees with undercut banks behind them and rocks near them. Great-looking trees hanging over water moving at high speed didn't hold a one!

Wherever there is moving water, always look for nearby protected hiding places. Fish don't want to swim 90 mph just to stay in one place.

They want to sit in quiet places and wait for food to be swept by. They'll dart out, grab it, and then swim back to their protected area.

Some seagoing ocean fish have no such sense, but are built for constant speed, as is the tuna. Did you know that the tuna has little indentations in its body to fold its fins into, so they don't create drag? It's just like putting a blade back into a penknife. What a high-speed design! It's the tuna sports car version.

QUESTION 15. DO OTHER FACTORS PRESENT IN THE WATER AFFECT LOCATION?

CHECKLIST
- Chemicals
- Nitrate/algae blooms
- Oxygen
- Suspended particles

In fishing, once you have exhausted all the possibilities, you must ask yourself "Is there anything else?" Often there is.

The first tournament I ever won was a dusk-to-dawn night tournament held by the Northern Bass Anglers Association on Lake Cochituate in Natick, Massachusetts. I won it because I asked myself "Is there anything else?" The key to the lake was very interesting indeed on August 13, 1976!

Fish in this lake were almost untouchable after dark, and nobody was sure why. I suspected it might have something to do with the lake's oxygen content. Many local homes had leeching systems that drained nitrogen-rich ooze into the lakeshore soil. This nitrogen, I believed, caused algae blooms in the shallow-water weed beds. Plants feed on nitrogen. Algae, which are microscopic plants, and the weeds in the lake create energy through photosynthesis. Photosynthesis makes oxygen in the sunlight and uses oxygen in the absence of sunlight. I surmised that the algae- and weed-rich weed beds that produced fish during the day would be devoid of fish or would have very slow-moving fish at night. Why? Because the fish had nothing to breathe! It was like trying to breathe on a high mountain peak, where the air is thin. Every slight motion would be an exertion.

I put this theory to the test. At night I fished those places that had no weeds, yet had a steep breaking shoreline from shallow to deep water. These places had more oxygen because they had no oxygen-depleting weeds. Did I win the tournament? You bet! And my partner (who was paired with me in the draw) came in second. It was a very tough tournament with many boats catching no fish at all. What I did was to figure out the key variable that let us catch those fish at night. Nobody else took the time to think about it! Did I have an oxygen meter to deduce this? No, I couldn't afford one at the time. I had to use my seat-of-the-pants wits and observational skills, combined with some basic knowledge. So can you.

Another interesting situation occurs on this lake and comes about from the same oxygen condition. The brighter the day, the better the fishing is! Cold front days are excellent, when they should bring poor fishing conditions. This flies in the face of all generalizations about weather. Why is this true? Because the brighter the day, the more sunlight there is to produce oxygen through photosynthesis from this pea-green soupy water. Oxygen coming into the water where there was none before overrides all other factors, including the negative effect of cold fronts on this particular lake. Cloudy days are generally not as good because there is not as much oxygen in the water.

Good ol' Lake Cochituate . . . I used to call it the crazy lake. If the algae situation hasn't changed, I'll bet the fish in the summer still act the same way—different!

The "Where" Questions

These questions will help you answer how the body of water itself that you are fishing on a given day will help determine where the fish will be *(place)*.

QUESTION 16. WHAT TYPE OF BODY OF WATER ARE YOU FISHING?

CHECKLIST

Freshwater
- Natural lake
- Swamp/bog
- Reservoir
- Enhanced lake
- Dishpan lake/farm pond
- Freshwater sea

- Canal
- Stream or river

Saltwater
- Ocean quadrant
- Ocean bay
- Canal
- Island/reef
- Saltwater lake

Brackish
- River/river mouth
- Bay
- Marsh area

Other

It is important to be aware of the kind of water you are fishing and the effect this has on the location of your quarry. I can't cover every type of water in detail here. You'll have to do your own research when you select where to fish, but here are some examples.

A natural lake has certain types of cover that hold fish. In general, the key to natural lakes is the weed cover. Fish tend to relate to weeds, wood, and caves. Deep dropoffs are not a big factor most of the year, except in the fall and winter. Don't bother looking for current in these lakes, except for stream run-ins and natural underwater springs. There also tend not to be many man-made obstructions on the bottom, as there are in reservoirs, which were dry before and then were flooded.

Reservoirs offer a wider variety of cover, such as creek channels (the original river channel before the reservoir was flooded), standing timber, and the fourth dimension, water current.

Saltwater is such a vast area that it is often best to deal with quadrants, or manageable areas. A quadrant might be the Elizabeth Islands near Martha's Vineyard. These islands are several miles long as well as wide. There are currents, tides, rips, and fish-hiding places that create a unique ecosystem in that area. Another quadrant might be Key West harbor in Florida, which has its own cover, seasonal timing, and so forth. Quadrants are manageable, whereas the vast ocean is overwhelming. Study each quadrant and make it your own. In the checklist, freshwater sea refers to vast areas of fresh water such as the Great Lakes or the Baikal Sea in Russia. Again, you must divide these lakes into manageable quadrants and learn all there is to know about these specific areas.

Brackish water is a mix between saltwater and freshwater and usually occurs in marshes near saltwater or where rivers enter the ocean. Depending on the tide, the salt content of these areas rises and falls. At times you can catch saltwater and freshwater species side by side. Imagine, after catching a few largemouth bass, you go to lip the next fish, and it's a razor-toothed bluefish. Careful!

Read as much as you can about the type of water you are fishing. Go through the checklist in the next question and identify the types of cover that are available to fish on that body of water. Then make your best selections when you answer Question 19.

QUESTION 17. WHAT ARE THE BEST LOCATIONS THAT THE FISH HAVE TO CHOOSE FROM IN THIS BODY OF WATER TO ACCOMMODATE LIVING AND FEEDING, GIVEN QUESTION 16.

CHECKLIST

Wood

- Trees
- Docks
- Pilings
- Any other wooden obstruction
- Standing timber

Rock

- Natural rocks
- Natural bluffs
- Riprap
- Bridge abutments
- Breakwaters/jetties
- Rock walls/dams

Natural Growth

- Weeds of all kinds
- Coral
- Overhanging trees/mangrove roots

Caves

- Undercut banks
- Culverts

- Bridges
- Bluff outcroppings, or lips

Contours
- Points
- Dropoffs
- Bars
- Humps
- Shallow feeding areas
- Any bottom contour features

Current
- Tides
- Eddies/pools/quiet areas
- Rips
- Dam-related current/water levels
- Wind and wave-induced current
- Industrial water inflows/outflows (e.g., power plants)

Submerged Cover
- Man-made structures/roadbeds
- Obstructions
- Underwater wrecks, rocks, etc.
- Debris
- Anything ever placed underwater by humans

Floating Objects
- Boats, barges
- Rafts, water-skiing ramps
- Debris, wood, trees
- Floating weeds, dead or alive

Other
- Fish suspension points in open water (e.g., thermoclines, temperature)
- Deep water troughs
- Shallow water troughs
- Any other visible or invisible factors in the environment that fish relate to

This is a quick checklist of the types of cover and structure that fish use, which I have discussed throughout this book. Check off the types of cover that are available where you're fishing. The next question narrows things down. Your body of water may contain even more or different types of cover. Is there any other unusual cover that isn't included here? Write it down and explore it.

QUESTION 18. IS THIS BODY OF WATER ABNORMAL IN ANY WAY? HOW WILL THIS AFFECT FISHING?

POSSIBILITIES

- It's tiny: Locations overlap seasons.
- It's huge: lake, waterway or ocean. Quadrants provide subenvironments to explore (e.g., reservoirs, St. Lawrence Seaway, ocean areas such as Florida Keys)

I have a saying, "All fishing is local." I borrowed it from former Speaker of the House Tip O'Neill, who once said, "All politics are local." That is to say, the only thing that matters on a given local body of water is what's there. Period. If the body of water is unusual, fish will adapt to what is available and make do.

One pike in Poland was sitting under some lily pads when vacationing Chris Musidowski from New Jersey, age twelve, threw a Flying Lure at it. He writes, "Thank you for inventing [the Flying Lure]. I couldn't believe my eyes when it went under the lily pads and did not get snagged. I caught a monster pike! I have $250.00 worth of fishing stuff and out of all of it, the Flying Lure was the only one to do the job." That pike used the available cover in the lake to hide and ambush-feed. Chris found the cover and caught the pike by sending a lure in there. Simple! Chris figured it out.

Tiny lakes such as farm ponds and golf course ponds are so small that often the minnows are hunchbacked. Now *that's* small! Because of the lack of available space and cover, fish must spawn and go through the winter in relatively the same places. Therefore, be aware that fish use the *same* cover at different times of the year for different reasons. They'll use a sunken tree to provide cover during the spawn and later, in the summer, will use the same tree to ambush minnows. In my early days of fishing, I thought I was doing something wrong, because I was catching fish from the same places in small ponds year round. According to the magazines, I was supposed to be catching them in different places. No one told me that this was the case in many smaller ponds—even in ponds that are several hundred acres in size! So, start with book theory, but be ready to believe your own senses and exploration. Whoever wrote the article you just read

Chris Musiolowski and his pike, caught on vacation in Poland. *(Courtesy Jacek Musiolowski)*

hasn't been to your pond. Once you've spent some fishing time there, you're probably more qualified to say what's really happening there. And keep answering the thirty-three Fishing Success Questions as they apply to that body of water. Soon you'll be the expert.

Always keep in mind any other abnormalities that would make this body of water behave unlike any other.

QUESTION 19. WHAT ARE THE TOP THREE PLACES TO FISH ON THIS BODY OF WATER TODAY?

That's the perennial question: "Where are they biting today?" Well, now you have the tools to figure it out. If you've gone through all of the *place* questions, you have narrowed the possibilities down considerably. And this is what we are really trying to do, eliminate unproductive water and focus in on the best water on a given day.

You know about the fish you are chasing. You know what time of the year it is. You know about the type of body of water you are fishing. You have identified the types of cover that are available on that body of water (Question 17 checklist). Given the fish's seasonal habits, you can deduce the best types of cover on that body of water at this time of year.

Now you should begin to ask as many local people as you can about where the fish are biting, to help you develop your own game plan. Never be afraid to ask! Asking doesn't mean you're stupid, it means that you are smart. Get rid of that ego!

What do touring pros do when they arrive at a lake? They get as much information as possible from local fishermen. Why? Because they don't know how to fish? I don't think so! It is because despite all the theories and books and magazines, all fishing is local. Nobody has better or more current information than somebody that's just been fishing at the time and place where you are. It's that simple.

Create your own notebook based on the thirty-three Fishing Success Questions and keep filling it in. Update it every time you go fishing. I promise you, *you* will be the expert in a very short period of time, because nobody else will make the effort. You will have more information than anyone else. People will be coming to you for advice. Knowledge is power. You will have the knowledge if you go out and get it.

7

Presentation

What Lures and Retrieves to Use

Presentation in regard to fishing is a term that I believe was first used by Al Lindner. Anglers often use the term to describe a lure's speed and retrieve.

Presentation, as I use the term here, refers to the color, size, and motion of the lure only—that is, how the lure "presents itself" to the fish. Based on different factors, the best presentation will change. The following questions will help steer you toward the correct presentation for the fish you're after.

QUESTION 20. AT THIS TIME OF YEAR, WHAT IS THE FISH'S PRIMARY FOOD SOURCE?

CHECKLIST

- Size
- Color
- Action, motion

"Matching the hatch" is a concept that trout fishermen are familiar with. It refers to using a fly that matches whatever type of insect that has just hatched on the stream. By matching the color and size of the fish's natural food, they increase their chances of catching a fish. The "matched" lure is part of the search image of a trout at that time of the year. As the year goes on, it will change. The size and color will change, and so forth.

Any fish, saltwater or freshwater, is more likely to strike a lure that is close to its natural search image. If tarpon off of Key West, Florida, are feeding on six- to nine-inch silver-colored fish in the spring, what do I use? A six- or nine-inch silver shad or white Flying Lure.

If brook trout in the Adirondack Mountains of New York are feeding on two- to three-inch crawfish and minnows, what should I be using? A 2-inch crawfish- or minnow-colored Flying Lure. I went on a trout-fishing trip with Don Meissner. Locals said that the only thing these educated brookies would take was a black-and-yellow fly. . . . Wrong! The two-inch Flying Lure matched the food of these fish at this time of year. At other times when surface hatches prevail, a dry fly or a surface-retrieved Flying Lure would do better. Preferably it would match the color and size of the hatch.

Even if you are fishing for nonpredators such as carp, always keep in mind the color and size and action of their natural food, and try to match its attributes.

QUESTION 21. HOW FAST WILL A FISH MOVE TO CHASE A LURE?

CHECKLIST

- Fish's metabolism at this time of year? (fast, slow, medium?)
- Desire to chase a lure at all.
- Speed of its preferred food source.

A fish's metabolism changes with the water temperature. This fact is often overlooked by fishermen who retrieve lures at the same speed year round. In the spring, for warm-water North American species, a medium-slow retrieve is necessary to keep in tune with the fish's medium-speed metabolism. In the summer any retrieve, from a super-slow falling worm to a ripped crankbait, is okay, since the fish has a faster metabolism to chase it. In superheated water, sometimes fish slow down again.

You must learn the preferred temperature range for your species and then learn how the retrieve of your lure should vary for every five- to 10-degree change. Not much has been written about the speed of a lure versus the activity level of a fish at a given time of year. Experiment on your own. This is an area that I am personally doing research in. As soon as I gather more information, I'll make it available publicly.

QUESTION 22. AT THIS TIME OF YEAR, DOES A FISH HAVE OTHER MOTIVATIONS BESIDES FEEDING THAT WOULD MAKE IT TAKE A BAIT OR A LURE?

Many people assume that fish bite things only because they wish to eat. This is false. If at any time of year we can make a fish strike a lure for reasons other than hunger, we should take advantage of it because it gives us more chances to catch that fish. Possibilities include spawning, anger/arousal/competition, and territoriality.

SPAWNING

Fish are generally more vulnerable than usual during the spawning cycle. Largemouth and smallmouth freshwater bass are notorious nest-protectors. Placing a lure on a nest one time or repeatedly, if necessary, can elicit a strike. The fish strikes the lure to remove it from the nest, not to eat it.

ANGER/AROUSAL/COMPETITION

A number of professional bass fishermen have developed systems for catching fish in the summertime that use the anger/arousal "hot buttons" of bass. Instead of finessing a bass into striking, they throw a fast-moving crankbait by it and try to pull the bait away from it as fast as possible. This is trying to make fish hit by using its reflex response. It's like pulling a string past a cat. Sometimes a cat will strike it without thinking—just to stop it from getting away. I believe this is a natural competetive predatory response, to stop possible prey from escaping.

I often use a similar technique with the Flying Lure in a testing tank, as many have seen on TV. The persistence of the Flying Lure can anger a fish into striking, just as well as it can entice it. Again, imagine dangling a string in a cat's face over and over. It'll either move away or take a swipe at it.

In the summertime, saltwater bluefish are known for gorging themselves on food, and sometimes even slashing it and not eating it. A bluefish that hits a lure thrown into a school may aim to maim that lure or simply to keep it away from other fish in the school. I've heard of freshwater smallmouth bass behaving in a similar manner.

Jarvis Taylor of Richmond, Virginia, figured it out and got two great bluefish to prove it. I'll bet those lures didn't come back in one piece, though!

Jarvis Taylor and two bluefish. *(Courtesy Brenda Taylor)*

TERRITORIALITY

Often you can get a fish to strike just by being too close to it. This is especially true of hiding fish that you can find under obstructions with the Flying Lure. I have caught hundreds of fish in this manner. I put the lure right into the cover where the fish was hiding. The fish's response was something like "Hey, you! Get out of my living room. Okay, now you've had it! I'm gonna punch you in the nose." When the fish punches my lure in the nose, I've got it. This territorial response can be found in fish year round. African fish called cichlids are especially territorial. North American fish are moderately territorial, but can be made to strike.

In summary, always be on the lookout for motivations in fish that do not involve food. Sometimes these reasons will be the most powerful. Explore this area.

QUESTION 23. HOW DOES THE COLOR, SIZE, AND ACTION OF THE LURE CHANGE BASED ON WEATHER CONDITIONS?

CHECKLIST

- Wind speed
- Precipitation
- Light penetration in the water
- Cold fronts
- Abnormal weather conditions

Weather has a great bearing on the selection of your lure.

WIND SPEED

The wind generally tells us more that we can't do something than that we can. For example, high wind conditions can prevent us from effectively fishing lures such as jigs because the wind prevents us from having proper contact with the lure through the line. The wind interferes by blowing the line all over the place. Working and feeling the lure becomes impractical. In times like these we must go to a heavier, castable lure, such as a plug or a spinner, that allows us to maintain a taut line all the time. This means that the lure must be retrieved constantly. Flying Lures can be worked with the rod tip uncharacteristically low, near the water's surface. Follow the action of the lure horizontally with your rod tip near the water's surface.

Wind creates water currents and blows some species of food fish against the shoreline, or rocks, or shoals. This can set up an interesting situation where predators come to feed on these fish. Here, matching the size and color of the food species is very important.

PRECIPITATION

Precipitation affects your lure selection in two ways. First, if the rain washes worms and insects into the water, matching these with a lure of similar color and size can be ideal.

More important, precipitation tends to make water more cloudy or dirty because of the natural erosion that takes place in freshwater and coastal areas. Dirtier water often means using larger, brighter-colored lures, so the fish can see them. It often also means a higher level of *persistence.* (See Question 31.)

LIGHT PENETRATION IN THE WATER

As weather relates to color, there are no hard and fast rules. Some people say "Bright days, bright lures. Dark days, dark lures." In many cases this is true. The *location* matters more, in my opinion, than weather or general rules. In bodies of water with similar characteristics, sometimes lure colors in the opposite ends of the spectrum are successful. In general, the higher the light penetration is in the water, the more natural the lure color should be. This doesn't necessarily mean darker. It simply means "matching the hatch" as closely as possible because the visual acuity of fish is higher in clear water than in dirtier water. This can mean browns and blacks as well as silvers, golds, and whites. Every fish prefers a slightly different offering.

On darker days I prefer darker lures that don't stand out like a sore thumb. Ask local anglers what colors are best on which days . . . and experiment. Many of the great new lure colors are discovered by accident, or because it was the only color you had left! Experiment with color.

Generally speaking, you use a smaller lure size on a very bright day than you would on a dark, windy day . . . but there are no hard and fast rules about size either. You must learn what works on your body of water under given weather conditions.

COLD FRONTS

Cold fronts tend to make fish more skittish than normal due to high light penetration in the water. Fish tend to take smaller, finesse lures in situations like this. Small natural lures, such as the Flying Lure, or small plastic worms or grubs, fished in a very natural manner, tend to work the best under these conditions. The converse is also true. One great fisherman that I know takes out a big crankbait and starts throwing it as hard and as fast as possible after a cold front. His strategy is to present the lure to as many fish as possible and make one strike out of a reflex response.

ABNORMAL WEATHER CONDITIONS

Always be aware of unseasonable or unusual weather. For example, an extreme cold front may reduce the size of an effective lure to only the tiniest jig. Likewise with a hot spell, which may deplete the oxygen content of shallow water. This situation may limit the angler to very slow-moving lures, cast into cover since fish may not move at all unless the lure is dropped right on its head.

QUESTION 24. HOW DO THE FACTORS FOUND IN WATER AFFECT THE COLOR, SIZE, SPEED, AND ACTION OF A LURE THAT WOULD BE ATTRACTIVE TO FISH?

CHECKLIST

- Water color
- pH
- Temperature
- Water current
- Oxygen content
- Chemicals

Water conditions heavily affect the selection of lure color and size.

WATER COLOR

In dirtier or stained water, I prefer to use the brighter, better-seen colors, also lures with "flash." For example, I prefer to use the Flying Lure in bright colors, such as chartreuse (bright yellow/green) with metalflake. Not only is the color of the lure visible, but the metalflake reflects any available light, like one of thôse disco balls above a dance floor. No wonder it makes fish dance in the dark! Lures that make sound by displacing water, such as spinnerbaits and crankbaits, are also preferred in dark water because they have the added dimension of fish attraction by noise. Placing a glass rattle inside the body cavity of the Flying Lure can replicate this.

In clear water, I use a considerably smaller lure than in dirty water. Natural colors are preferable in clear water, in my opinion, because fish can see well. We're trying to mimic food more than attracting the fish to know that we're there at all.

PH

Ph can affect your lure choice. The closer the Ph to your fish's preferred range the more active the fish will be. Active fish are more likely to chase moving lures. Likewise, any pollutants or unnatural irritants in the water will damage a fish's ability to chase a fast-moving lure. In general, anything that causes instability in the water will affect the choice of lures.

TEMPERATURE

Water temperature is a simple and effective guide for lure presentation. The colder the water, the slower your lure presentation should be. The higher the temperature, the faster the lure should be retrieved. The relative speeds of the lure depend on the species you're fishing for.

The Flying Lure has an optimum swimming speed built in, to trigger strikes all year—in July as well as through the ice in January. The reason? It swims at the speed of an injured minnow as it goes under cover. This slow-falling speed attracts fish all year. As far as I know, this type of super-slow fall is about the only retrieve that is perfect for catching fish year round, in ice-cold or warm water. That's why I built it in to the lure!

The only advice I have is to work your Flying Lure faster on the retrieve back to you during warm-water periods.

OTHER FACTORS IN THE WATER

Other factors in the water, such as the presence of oxygen, can have a direct bearing on the presentation of your lure. If oxygen is depleted in a certain lake or area, smaller lures and slower retrieves are in order. This condition often happens in the summertime, when algae blooms in lakes and reservoirs take place. When this happens, fish can slow down because of the lack of oxygen in the water. Remember your goldfish gasping for air in the bowl when you were a kid? It's a very similar situation to this. Fish just aren't going to be active and chasing fast-moving large lures. They're out of breath!

At times, the water current has a direct bearing on your presentation because it may force you to use a larger lure, if you're going to fish at all. In this case, you either go fish somewhere else or fish with a lure that's bigger than what you really want, just so the water current won't blow it away.

QUESTION 25. WHAT IS THE BEST LURE FOR THIS BODY OF WATER?

CHECKLIST

- Primary forage fish
- Special conditions in this body of water (e.g., heavy weeds, current, etc.)
- "Hot" color

How does the body of water affect your lure choice? First of all, the predominant food species will set a preferred size and color range of lure. If the predominant minnow or shiner that largemouth bass feed on in a particular lake is four inches long, your lure selection should be similar. If smallmouth bass are feeding on two- to three-inch crawfish, then a two- or four-inch Flying Lure in root beer or crawfish color is a good choice.

Some lakes just seem to have hot colors. It's lime green on some, red on others, pink on still others. There is no particular rhyme or reason for this except that whatever combination of *where* and *water* factors existing on that body of water dictate a specific color that fish are attracted to.

Be on the lookout for special conditions that may indicate lure selection on this body of water. Is there an inordinate amount of moss? Do you have to penetrate it with a heavier six-inch Flying Lure, or a five-eighths–ounce jig? Are there vast stump fields that are best explored with a spinnerbait?

Always look for those special conditions on a body of water that may be subtle but unique to it. That's where you can have an edge over others who may be good but don't know the intricacies of the water as well as you do.

8

Proximity

I use the term proximity to refer to how close a lure must be to a fish to get a reaction. Imagine a fish in the water. Now, looking from the top down, draw a circle around that fish, let's say three feet in diameter. It's really an irregular sphere, not a circle, but you get the picture. Let's call that the *proximity* within which your lure has to be to draw a reaction. That's the playing field! You can't score outside of it.

To put it another way, you're the baseball pitcher and that's your strike zone. The fish is the batter. If you put the lure over the plate you'll get a strike (from a fish), or you'll pitch a ball (no strike). The proximity is the size of the strike zone today. In fishing, unlike baseball, it changes daily. What a game!

And, by the way, the fish set the rules. How does it make you feel, to play by a fish's rules? (Although the fish are probably smarter than some umpires.) Okay, now let's go play baseball!

QUESTION 26. HOW FAR WILL A FISH MOVE TO TAKE YOUR LURE FROM WHERE IT IS AT THIS TIME OF YEAR?

Based on the season, the strike zone *(proximity)* of many fish changes. Seasonally, the effects on proximity can be boiled down to:

- Water temperature
- Biological needs (e.g., spawning)
- Available cover

As water temperature rises, fish become more aggressive and likely to chase after a lure. Their proximity zone increases. As water temperature decreases, they will have a smaller proximity zone.

For example, largemouth bass have a small proximity zone in the wintertime. They are on the deeper drops in a lake and are not likely to chase a bait very far. In the spring, as the bass prepare to spawn, their proximity zone increases. They are likely to respond to a lure, depending on other conditions, over a much larger area, let's say ten to fifteen feet when active. When they are actually on the spawning beds, their proximity zone is about the size of home plate in an actual ballpark. If your lure isn't on the plate (their spawning bed), you're out! In the summer the zone gets much wider as the temperature increases and the metabolism of the bass does likewise.

Understand the seasonal proximity of your quarry as a guideline. For example, in the wintertime, don't waste your time making long, quick casts with a crankbait. Find the places where the fish are with a sonar and make lots of pinpoint casts to that area until you bump the fish on the head.

A letter that I received from Paul Webster, Jr., illustrated this point perfectly.

> Recently my grandfather . . . purchased a [Flying Lure] kit for me to try out. I couldn't wait for the coming weekend, so I woke my wife up and we headed for my uncle's catfish pond. . . . I started to throw my Weed Walker, Rattle Traps, Chatterbox, spinnerbaits, and six or eight different [plastic] worms. With my plastic worms, I worked a cedar tree that had been sunk out in the pond. The only problem was that I could never get under the cedar tree.
>
> Finally, I put on my six-inch electro blue Flying Lure. On the second cast at the tree, I lifted my rod up and [let] it back down. The next thing I know, I had one big strike. I set the hook firmly and started to reel it in. My wife was yelling because it was the biggest bass she has ever seen. It turned out to be the biggest bass I have ever caught. The bass weighed 5.8 pounds. I want to congratulate you on such a wonderful lure. I am enclosing a picture of the fish I caught.

Paul Webster, Jr., and his biggest bass ever. *(Courtesy Paul Webster)*

Look at all the factors here. Paul put it all together. It was a cold February in Texas. He had to have a very tight proximity. The "rattle" baits and spinnerbaits did not work because the bass were not chasing. They were hunkered down in their winter pattern. Even plastic worms did not have the proximity because they couldn't get under the tree. The Flying Lure had the necessary proximity and got a fish! Also, note that the six-inch size was appropriate because the bass were used to feeding on larger fish (catfish). The color was a good reflective color for the murky water conditions that catfish ponds often have. I think the fact that the lure was hit on the second fall meant that it also had to have some persistence that the other lures did not have. Nice job, Paul!

Outdoor writer Rich Zaleski once won the Northern Bass Anglers

Association Championship in November of 1978 by finding a school of fish in deep water and sitting on them for two days. By making lots of slow, almost motionless pinpoint casts, he won hands down. Those fish were hunkered down and not moving for anybody, except for Rich . . . veeeery slooowly. The lure had to be dropped on their heads.

In warmer water, the proximity zone expands, and you are free to make faster, longer casts and cover more water in the anticipation of at least some chasing fish. In the Florida Keys, I believe the proximity of an active barracuda can be 100 feet or more. What does that mean? Make lots of casts and cover lots of water.

QUESTION 27. UNDER THESE WEATHER CONDITIONS, HOW CLOSE MUST YOUR LURE BE TO THE FISH TO GET A REACTION?

CHECKLIST

- Wind causing turbulence
- Precipitation causing cloudy water
- Cold fronts causing nonchasing fish
- A sudden temperature shock to the surface (hot or cold)

Wind and rain often cause turbulence in the water and reduce the proximity zone. Turbulence causes a disturbance in the sound as well as in the visual area. In the pounding surf, a lure can be missed more easily than in a tiny pond. By the way, you can see why it's important not to create a disturbance when you're fishing a small, quiet pond: Your body may be *in* the proximity zone if you're wading.

The practical application of this information is to make more and closer casts when there is turbulence or water discoloration. Remember, each cast strains the water. Each cast is a strand in your imaginary net. You need more strands closer together when proximity is reduced by turbulence or discoloration.

Rain can also cause a shock to the shallow water by dropping the temperature several degrees after a rainfall. The change in temperature will reduce the likelihood of fish being active and chasing anything.

Cold fronts are usually a nemesis as well. They make fish retreat and stay close to their cover. Cold-front fish sometimes have the proximity of a postage stamp! After a cold front, find the best cover you can and fish it with pinpoint casts of a Flying Lure. Probe each area a number of times until you hit the fish on the head.

QUESTION 28. HOW DOES THE WATER AFFECT THE DISTANCE THAT A FISH WILL TRAVEL TO STRIKE A LURE?

CHECKLIST

- Water current
- pH
- Temperature
- Oxygen
- Chemicals

In general, the more things that make a fish uncomfortable in the water, the less it will be inclined to move to strike a lure.

Water current tends to concentrate fish. The more current, the greater the concentration of fish, the closer you must get the lure to where the fish are hiding. Fortunately, the Flying Lure can penetrate the eddies, crevices, and undercuts where fish hide and swim right in there.

Unusual conditions, such as wrong pH for the species or chemicals in the water, or anything that is a shock to the system, tends to decrease the proximity zone.

A lower temperature tends to decrease the proximity zone (see Question 26); higher temperatures tend to increase it.

Low oxygen content in the water due to hot temperatures (warm water holds less dissolved oxygen than cold water) tends to decrease the proximity zone in many species of fish, such as bass, pike, and trout. For these fish species, abundant oxygen tends to increase the zone.

In some of the sessions I do at fish tanks in public places, native fish have been caught and brought in to the tank the night before. The fish handlers and tank personnel are professionals and take care of the fish exceptionally well—even to the point of disinfecting them! Even so, many of the variables are a shock to the fish—new water, lights, people, and so forth. For the first few days, the proximity zone of some of these fish is one *inch* or less! I've actually watched a slow-motion replay of this. If you don't land the lure right on its nose—I mean exactly one inch away or closer—it won't take the lure. Of course, I don't use hooks while fishing in a tank, I just tease the fish.

MORE ABOUT CATCH AND RELEASE

A word about catch and release. The fish that you see me "playing with" in the tank on TV have usually been caught by local fishermen from a local lake on hook and line in the past day. The fact that we can play with them shows how healthy and active fish can be just hours after actually being caught in the wild and released into a tank. Hooks, which are now surgically sharp, make a small hole in the fish's jaw area and are easily removed. Catch and release works and is humane when using artificial lures (which fish don't tend to swallow) with a single, sharp hook, which makes a single tiny incision in a nonvulnerable area.

QUESTION 29. HOW CLOSE TO THE FISH DOES A LURE HAVE TO BE IN A THIS BODY OF WATER?

CHECKLIST

- The fish's level of skittishness (In some lakes, fish are more skittish than others, for whatever reason.)
- Availability and type of cover
- Amount of wind or turbulence
- Other local factors affecting proximity

Some bodies of water have chasing fish, others have more timid, nibbling fish. Proximity, which is lake specific is best determined by trial and error. Often, proximity differences among bodies of water tend to be related more to the cover that is available and the water clarity.

Cover, such as heavy weeds, affects the proximity zone by segregating fish in weed pockets. You have to hit the pockets or weed clumps. Otherwise, the fish won't move to get your lure.

Water clarity, discussed in Question 27, tends to increase the proximity zone. Turbid or dirty water tends to make the zone smaller because the fish can't see as well.

Fishing pressure is the great variable of our time. As fishing becomes increasingly popular, pressure is increased on just about every body of water. Increased pressure brings fewer chasing fish. A lack of pressure brings some wildly chasing fish! I haven't experienced a near-virgin lake in at least fifteen years. I hope there are still some left.

9

Persistence

How Frequently the Fish Must See the Lure

After I invented the Flying Lure, I began to use the term persistence to describe the action of multiple presentations by a single lure. The term refers to the Flying Lure's ability to act like a pushy salesman—that is, going into a fish's face again and again. It turns out that this is perhaps the most important attribute for a lure to have in order to catch inactive fish. And fish are inactive most of the time. My definition of inactive is not actively feeding and either neutrally or negatively disposed to striking any lure.

QUESTION 30. HOW MANY TIMES MUST THE LURE ACTIVELY APPROACH THE FISH BEFORE IT STRIKES AT THIS TIME OF YEAR? HOW LONG MUST THE FISH BE IN VISUAL CONTACT WITH THE LURE BEFORE IT STRIKES?

The season affects persistence because fish behave differently, mostly due to water temperature and their biological clock. To take the example of a largemouth bass, the cooler the water, the higher the lure's persistence has to be. In the cooler months you often have to tease a bass to come out of its hiding place. In the fall, when the water starts to cool rapidly, multiple presentations to the same piece of cover are at times imperative. Before the Flying Lure was invented, I remember having to make five, ten, or even twenty casts to a piece of cover that I knew was good, to move a bass into striking. With the Flying Lure, you can make multiple presentations instantly without recasting. Also, when fish are less active, continually throwing a lure into the water and having it splash down is like throwing rocks in the water. It is unnatural and can disturb the fish. Also, you probably aren't casting the lure into exactly the same place time after time. Inches count when fish are skittish! Multiple pinpoint, soft presentations by the Flying Lure solve the problem.

In the case of bedding smallmouth bass, persistence can be the only key in getting them to hit. Every time the lure swims back to the nest, the fish becomes more aroused (or angry). After the fifth or nineteenth time a seemingly uninterested fish can be yours. It won't seem that way at first, but try it sometime. It works.

In general, colder water due to seasonality means more persistence is required. Warmer water often means that less persistence is required. When fish are territorial, such as during the spawn, persistence can be the whole ball game. Color and size might hardly matter, as in the case of the smallmouth.

QUESTION 31. GIVEN THE WEATHER THAT EXISTS, WILL THE FISH BE PREDISPOSED TO STRIKE AGGRESSIVELY, OR MUST THE LURE MAKE MULTIPLE APPROACHES BEFORE THE FISH WILL STRIKE?

CHECKLIST

- Level of the stability index
- Existence of a cold front
- A temperature shock to the water

The less stability there is in the fish's environment, the more skittish it will be, and the more persistence it will require.

If the stability index is high, (see Question 8), then the persistence required of a lure will be lower. Fish will tend to take the lure more readily in a stable environment and will need less coaxing.

If the stability index is low, then persistence will have to be high. For example, if a cold front just came through, then fish will be very close to cover and often need a high degree of persistence to be caught. The Flying Lure really shines in tough, unstable environments because not only does it have persistence, but it has a perfectly natural fall for nonaggressive fish. Also, the very act of persistence has a 180-degree change of direction built into it. This change of direction is a powerful strike trigger.

QUESTION 32. HOW DOES THE WATER AFFECT THE NUMBER OF TIMES THAT A FISH NEEDS TO HAVE A LURE PRESENTED TO IT BEFORE IT STRIKES?

CHECKLIST

- Temperature
- Oxygen
- pH
- Chemicals

As discussed in Question 30, generally, as water temperature rises, the necessary persistence often drops. But instability in weather, no matter the water temperature, makes persistence rise again. So, during a hot summer, as a small cold front comes through an area, persistence will be high, despite a warm water temperature. As water temperature keeps rising past 75° to 80°, many species will suffer from oxygen depletion and superheating. In this case, persistence rises again, because fish are less active and mobile. The fish are less active because there is less dissolved oxygen in warmer water, and they are outside of their temperature comfort range.

Any instability in the water, including pH or chemical, tends to increase the need for persistence over that of a stable environment. Relatively speaking, stable water conditions decrease the need for persistence.

QUESTION 33. HOW MANY TIMES MUST A FISH SEE A LURE BEFORE IT STRIKES IN THIS BODY OF WATER?

In general, if a body of water is unstable in its water currents, weather patterns, and water composition, it will require a higher level of persistence than a similar body of water that has stability on all fronts.

The effect of humans on fish has to be considered in determining this question. Rick Clunn, four-time Bass Masters Classic winner, stated that people create "pressure zones" through fishing pressure that fish actively try to escape. It has been proven that fish will actually move away from places that are heavily fished. The Flying Lure can be fished in the "no-pressure" zones where other lures cannot go—under the heaviest cover. Once you get the lure into a no-pressure zone, it seems fish are so surprised to see an an intruder in their living room that they attack it immediately.

WHAT ABOUT THE DEMONSTRATION TANKS?

Consider the large glass tanks that I often demonstrate the lures in, such as the Hawg Trough. The conditions here, although healthy for the fish, are unstable from the fish's point of view—new water, changing light conditions, changing water temperature, and so forth. Here one of the keys to catching these fish when they are skittish is persistence. That's why Flying Lures are so effective in these situations—because they have persistence and stay right in the fish's face. Other lures can't. That's one of the reasons why I do so well in these tanks time after time, year after year.

We've come to the end of our Fishing Success Questions. But it's

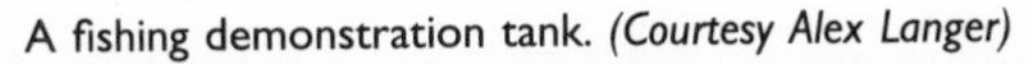

A fishing demonstration tank. *(Courtesy Alex Langer)*

really just the beginning! If you become a student of them, they will point you toward the path of success. In the remaining chapters of the book we'll be discussing the attitudes and action steps of putting it all together. We'll discuss how you can transfer the knowledge you gain by answering the thirty-three Fishing Success Questions into action.

10

Winning Attitudes/ Losing Attitudes

The Success Habits of the Pros

The greatest fishermen I know seldom have the most elaborate theories. But they are masters at putting together a lot of simple facts and coming up with a simple game plan that catches fish. That's it.

Winning Attitudes Versus Losing Attitudes

To be a winner in the sport of fishing, you must have the right attitude. In fact, attitude is the most important element a fisherman can bring to the water. On any given day on any given lake, there are winners and there are losers. You can see this especially at a tournament's weigh-in. If you ask the top five fishermen what happened today, you'll get totally different answers from those of some of the "also rans." You would swear that they were talking about different lakes entirely. But the lake was the same and the fish were the same, only the attitudes were different. With one attitude, a body of water can be a stern, unproductive place. With another, it can be a fascinating learning experience that leads to fishing success.

This is not to say that attitude alone will make you catch fish. It won't. But basic knowledge *plus* the right attitude will put you far ahead of someone with a lot of knowledge and an attitude that prevents him from using the knowledge to its fullest. That's why many new or young fishermen quickly surpass older, more knowledgeable people. They seek, question, experiment, and adapt . . . and don't get rattled by what seems like failure. Failure is a matter of opinion. Failure is at least 50 percent of my success. Let me explain.

Trial and Error
A Law of the Universe

Whether you like it or not, fishing is trial and error. You may stack some of the odds in your favor ahead of time by doing some research, or having a plan, or knowing the species you are fishing for, but when push comes to shove and you are on the water, it's trial and error. You really start figuring out what's going on when you catch the first fish, and the second, . . . so why is failure good?

Here's the anatomy of a fishing trip. You select a place to fish. You pick a lure. You make cast. You either catch a fish or you don't. You make the next cast. You either catch a fish or you don't. And so it goes.

Every cast has a result associated with it—catching a fish or not. If you don't catch a fish, it's a message for you to begin changing your tactics. Not immediately, but over time. A success tells you to keep doing what you're doing. It's a great feeling. But if you keep succeeding at what you're doing, it decreases your possibilities. It decreases your reality testing. If you've got "the answer," why look elsewhere? Why seek new and better methods? Failure is the other half of the equation. It tells you what to steer away from, but not exactly where to go. This is a challenge.

I often feel that a moderate success is sometimes a worse result than a total failure, because a moderate success lets us be complacent with a second-class result. It's like looking for a parking space at the mall. If you see one right away when you drive into the parking lot, but it's not very close to the door, you may take it just because it's good enough. If you don't see any spaces, you will be spurred on to keep looking for the very best space available. With the extra effort, you'll usually find one much closer to where you want to go. You won't settle for a second-class space because there wasn't one. Your options were to choose between a first-class space and failure. And now, from malls back to fishing. . . .

A failure tells you to get creative and change what you are doing. Failure makes you think. It expands your boundaries. Failure shouldn't be a message to keep on going. Failure is a call to thinking. Instead of calling what happens a failure, we should really call it a successful result that tells us what not to do.

The Flying Lure was invented out of a failure in fishing, not out of a success. I was skunked for two days in a row in a tournament. Pretty lousy, huh? It was humiliating. I thought I was a good fisherman . . . but after that tournament, I had my doubts. If I had been successful, I would never have invented the Flying Lure. If the fish weren't hiding under the deepest cover, which I couldn't get to, I could have won the tournament, but I wouldn't have invented the Flying Lure.

Failure made me think. It made me become creative. Failure made me determined to find a way to get to those fish that I couldn't get to before. I was forced to cut up some soda cans and melt some worms together so they would swim away from me and right into the fish's hiding place. Thank God I didn't win that tournament in 1977! Who would have remembered it? But it turns out that lots of people had the same fishing problems that I did and welcomed a new way to solve them. Hence the Flying Lure was born. Now it's the single best-selling lure in the world. It was a fifteen-year overnight success! I sure didn't see it that way in 1977, when I sat dejected at the weigh-in of that NBAA tournament on a hot July day, with a tune from *Saturday Night Fever* playing on my car radio. And who won that tournament? I honestly don't remember!

Everything Is Positive!

Rick Clunn, who is perhaps the greatest bass fishing champion of all time, with four Bass Masters Classic world championships to his credit, once explained his attitude to me. In his mind, Rick counts as positive everything that he encounters on the water. They are opportunities to learn and to steer him toward success. Rick never allows himself to become rattled and therefore short-circuit the creative process.

"What about getting your lure hung up in a tree?" I asked him. "Is that positive?" I thought I had him now! "Absolutely!" he replied. He went on to explain how most people would become frustrated at a hang-up and would stop thinking and learning. In a number of cases, Rick has caught fish and discovered new areas by bringing his boat close to shore to unhook his lure. He observed something in the shallow water that he wouldn't have seen otherwise. "I was able to discover new things about that body of water that I never would have discovered, had I not gotten hung up," Rick said calmly. Wow! What an attitude!

Even if a competitor goes to a spot that Rick was fishing on a previous day and gets there before him, Rick considers this an opportunity to fish another area that he wouldn't have fished at that time. I'd be furious! Maybe that's why he's the best in the world at what he does.

This reminds me of an attitude that I use in business. Whatever happens, negative or positive, I always say to myself, "Where's there an opportunity here? Where is there an advantage?" There are opportunities everywhere, in all kinds of circumstances. There are opportunities in defeat as well as success. This kind of self-talk is important to who you are and who you want to become. You are who you say you are—excited, frustrated, successful, or a failure. You define your opportunities or frustrations. We are all given the same lake to fish. Our attitude will make us master the circumstances or be ruled by them. It's our choice.

Losing Attitude: Failure to Adapt

Rick Clunn says that a fishing trip should be planned in advance. You should learn about the body of water you'll be fishing and about your quarry. But once you get there, you should be ready to adapt at a moment's notice.

Fishing is like going on a car trip. We can plan it by the road map, but when we actually start out, we may encounter conditions that may make us change our plans. For example, a section of highway may be under construction, and we may have to take an alternate route. What driver would plow through the barriers and demand to use the unfinished highway? Well, maybe a few of you would! But the rest would seek another way to get to their goal.

In fishing, it seems that most people want to plow through the barrier. I believe that at least half of the people on a given lake on a given day are fishing for yesterday's fish, with a lure that worked under a different set of weather and water conditions. They're fishing their favorite top-water method, when another lure fished deeper would be the key. Why? Because change is hard. You have to start thinking. They'd rather plow through the highway barrier and drive off an incomplete bridge than to stop and think of an alternate route. They aren't learning from failure. They're ignoring it! They aren't looking at failure as a positive reinforcement of what not to do.

World champion Rick Clunn: The "winningest" bass fisherman of all time. *(Courtesy Jim Caldwell)*

If something isn't working, *stop!* Assess what you are doing. Review the Fishing Success Questions, talk to other fishermen, fish shallower or deeper, or do something! One definition of insanity is to continue with the same activity, which has proved to bring you one result, and hope that it yields a different result. It's the ultimate pounding of your head against the wall.

When you first go out on a lake, experiment with different colors and sizes of lures, locations, and retrieves. Go through all of the possibilities on a given day. Don't just stick with one or two. When you start catching fish, stay with that pattern. When you stop catching fish, start to experiment again.

More Losing Attitudes

Ego is a great leveler in fishing. Ego makes you incapable of learning from others or even from failure. I have seen many local anglers get beaten on their home waters by traveling pros in a tournament. Instead of learning, some make excuses, such as "They front-ended me [didn't let me fish the good water at the front of the boat]," or "They were fishing their own waters and wouldn't take me to my spots," or "They were fishing for small fish. I only fish for big fish." When someone "cleans your clock" in fishing—and it's been done to me many times—swallow your pride and ask what he or she was doing. Most people will be glad to tell you, because it puts them in the driver's seat and they can bask in the glow of their success. Let them bask! You should learn, and then use that knowledge another day. Nobody catches fish all the time!

Bill Miller, a young man from Escondido, California, showed a great attitude when confronted with just such a situation. Here's a letter he wrote to me:

> Dear Alex,
>
> I've seen your show on TV and I was impressed, but I needed more. I heard that my friend had purchased the Flying Lures. We went to one of the local lakes called Lake Hodges. . . . We got there at about 6:10 and got our float tubes on the water. We fished with plastics of all kinds and we tried spinnerbaits and Fat Raps. I myself caught about four bass. As this day was coming to an end, I noticed that my friend wasted me in the time we fished. He even caught some very nice crappie and sunfish [on the Flying Lure].
>
> I bought my own set of lures, and took them up to one of the local

Bill Miller with a catch of California trout. *(Courtesy Bill Miller)*

lakes that had trout. I not only caught my limit, but caught some nice sized ones [using the two-inch chartreuse color]. I am sending a picture of this day. I also limited out on the two-inch black Flying Lure on Crappie!

Sincerely,
Bill Miller

P.S. Thanks. These lures work great.

Bill didn't get defensive about getting beaten in fishing by his friend. He turned it into a victory for himself by learning. As a result, he's catching more and bigger fish than before. It's a method that will probably serve him for years to come.

More Winning Attitudes

To sum it all up, as long as you keep an open mind, are willing to learn, and have a quiet confidence that is not rattled by circumstances, you have the most important tools to becoming an excellent fisherman. The bottom line is catching fish. Fish care only about whether you have the 4 P's right: *place, presentation, proximity,* and *persistence.* They care whether the lure is in front of their face in a way that appeals to them. That's it. They don't care about you, your ego, the size of your boat, the brand of reel that you are using, or what club you belong to.

The Best Advice of All

Above all, *have fun.* That's what fishing is all about. It's not deadly serious, and it's not all that important. Keep it all in perspective. You'll be happier that way.

11

How to Catch Your First Fish

Fishing with Kids and Novices

One of the greatest pleasures I have is to get a letter from a young person, or from a proud parent, reporting that the child caught a fish using a Flying Lure or some method I taught. That makes it all worth it to me. I remember the sense of awe I had as a child catching a fish, any fish. In fact, I remember the first fish I ever caught. It was a sunfish. But to me it was huge, beautiful, full of color, and shining like the sun. That awe has stayed with me all these years. I can remember every detail. Adults can recapture that awe the first time they catch a fish . . . or the first time they catch a fish in twenty or thirty years . . . since they were kids.

But how do you best start off a person on the road to catching a fish? What I have tried to do with the Flying Lure system is to make it the easiest lure in the world to use. It's a lure that you can literally give to kids, let them sit on a dock with a few feet of line, and they'll have a reasonable chance of catching a fish. I have many testimonials to this effect.

I would recommend that a beginner use a two-inch Flying Lure in any lake that is relatively clear. If the body of water is dingy or is saltwater, I would recommend the four- or six-inch version.

The reason I recommend a two-inch lure is that just about anything that swims will attack it—from a sunfish, to a snook, to a bass, to a forty-plus-pound muskellenge! Don Meissner lost what we believe would have been a line-class world-record musky on four-pound test line and a two-inch Flying Lure. We have that monster on videotape, though. Imagine, a four-foot-long fish hitting a two-inch lure.

What we're trying to instill in a novice or a child is a sense of confidence, a sense of "I can do this!" Otherwise, that person may be lost, never to try fishing again. Therefore, a two-inch lure has the highest probability of being hit by *something.* My personal saying is, If it doesn't hit a two-inch Flying Lure, it's probably dead!

I would recommend giving a novice a spinning or spin-casting rod of five to six feet in length, loaded with four- to six-pound test line. I realize that this is very light, but I want to maximize that person's chances of catching a fish. For the four-inch lure, I would recommend ten- to twelve-pound line. For the six-inch lure, I'd go with twelve- to fourteen-pound test.

All you want that person to do is to cast the lure toward any likely fish-holding cover that you can see from the surface. This can be a dock, a tree, weeds . . . anything. I promise you, if you do that long enough with a two-inch lure, you're bound to catch something! Why? Because I have just given you a shortcut. You say, I thought that there weren't any shortcuts in fishing. Well . . . there aren't, but this is as close as it gets.

Let's look at why this method works so well with novices in light of the 4 P's of the Flying Lure Success System.

Place

In any body of water at most times of the year, visible cover or weeds create shade. Whether the water is fresh or salt, that shade will hold either game fish or smaller food fish. If there is one immutable law of place, it is that if you find shade, you'll generally find some form of fish no matter what the season is. The easiest shade or cover for a novice to find is that which is visible from our world and yet has an impact on the fish's world. Get it? We start with baby steps.

At this point, the person starts to differentiate between cover that works and cover that doesn't work. He may find out that in this lake, boat docks don't hold nearly as many fish as sunken trees. As he fishes more, he may discover that the sunken trees are not all prime fishing water. Those in deeper water tend to hold more fish. As the new fisherman keeps learning and reading, he now has the confidence to discover new areas and try new things.

When I was a kid, nobody ever went out on a limb and said go here, use this, try this. I had to figure out how to apply articles I had read to my home lake . . . and that took some doing. I learned by trial and error and failure. Maybe that was okay too, since I had the desire at the beginning, which others may not have.

Presentation

I discussed earlier why the presentation of the Flying Lure, especially the two-inch lure, was so deadly. Specifically, it is small enough to entice any fish that swims, from the smallest to the largest, although Don Meissner found out that you may not be able to hold on to the largest fish that the two-inch lure can attract.

I believe that the single most important advantage of the Flying Lure for the novice is the fact that the lure fishes itself! As long as the fisherman can cast, lob, or even throw the lure into the water, it will give a perfect presentation every time. It will act as perfectly natural, enticing prey, totally free from human intervention. As long as the user gives the lure slack line and lets it sink to the bottom, the lure will work as it was designed in the factory. It will swim like a perfectly natural body in the water. Fish will respond to it as if it's alive. Most new fishermen have no clue how to work a lure. It takes many months to learn how to work the average lure properly. The Flying Lure will work itself like an expert on the first cast. All the fisherman has to do is to lift the rod tip one to three feet and release the lure again to swim on its own. If you have seen the Flying Lure infomercial, remember that 99 percent of the fish you see strike the lure do so as it is swimming on its own, not when it is being retrieved. It is catching fish on its own. I'm not controlling it when it is being hit. If there's a magic to this lure, that's it! It really does fish itself.

Even more than being totally natural, the lure possesses a strike trigger. Fisherman have observed that a change in the direction of a lure triggers strikes in fish. Changing the direction of a crankbait just a few degrees often works wonders. The Flying Lure does it better by reversing itself a full 180 degrees every time you pull it back and release it. A following fish is induced to strike it.

Less casting skill is required when you are approaching cover. If you just get it near the cover, the lure will slip under the cover on its own.

Proximity

No matter what the appropriate proximity of a lure is to the fish on a given day, closer is always better. When dealing with the type of surface-visible cover that we're discussing, no lure can get closer than one that goes right into a fish's hiding place. This is where the Flying Lure helps a novice tremendously. It just gets closer to the fish than other lures.

Persistence

After years of experimentation with the Flying Lure, I discovered that persistence is one of the keys to catching fish in the state they are normally in: Inactive! Inactive fish need a lure that keeps acting like a pushy salesman. It keeps going back in their face until they either take it out of hunger ("Oh, what the heck, I'll have this pesky morsel since

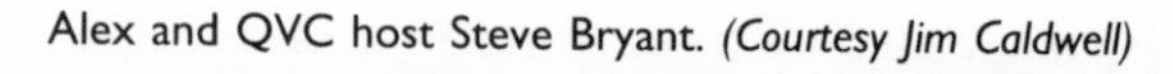
Alex and QVC host Steve Bryant. *(Courtesy Jim Caldwell)*

it's been in my face for the eighth time''), or they'll take it out of anger/arousal (''I'll swat this fly that's been making a pest of itself''). We now have two possible strike triggers, food and anger.

An Unparalleled Combination of Advantages

Finally, since there is no exposed lead on the lure, it feels soft to the touch—just like a real fish. That's the idea! Fish will hold on to the lure.

Don Meissner once did a TV show on lake trout with the Flying Lures. These trout were actually trying to swallow these lures, unlike most artificial lures. When we fish with the hookless lures in testing tanks, most of the bass will do the same thing. They'll swim around with the lures in their mouths until I pull them out. The lures are soft, hollow, and feel alive and, unlike most lures, there are no hard surfaces or exposed metal to spook the fish. What's the benefit here? For novices, it gives them time to set the hook or to realize that the fish is pulling the line away. Detecting strikes (feeling that elusive bump on the line) is often a big stumbling block for novices. It takes especially long to learn how to fish conventional soft plastics.

With the Flying Lure, feeling the strike is a bit less important as long as the fish continues to hold on until the angler is aware of its presence.

If you take a look at these advantages, they stack the cards in favor of the novices as never before. They can make the lure do what others in their experience range can't do with conventional lures or even with live bait. They can use the strike triggers and natural action built into the lure and put it into the very best fish hiding places in a lake.

Will novices catch fish every time? Of course not. Nobody catches fish all the time. But will they catch more fish with the Flying Lure? Yes, I believe they will, because for the first time, the cards are stacked in their favor.

Story after story is sent in and phoned in about kids and first-timers catching fish. Here are just a few I thought you might enjoy.

The Fifth ''P'': Proof

Jim Perkerson, a twelve-year-old angler, wrote to me recently. He said:

> Thank you so much for the Flying Lure. I enjoyed the heck out of it. I first saw the Flying Lure on TNN TV broadcasting. I thought that this

Jim Perkerson and his seventeen-inch bass. *(Courtesy Kevin Stiuzzieri)*

Carolyn's husband with his first bass ever caught on the Flying Lure. *(Courtesy Carolyn Platt)*

> lure was a great idea. When I told my dad about it he said it was a gimmick, but I still had faith. I begged and pleaded until he finally budged. . . .
>
> Three weeks later I was on spring break in Sandestin Beach, Florida. Our condo was on a golf course . . . and there were plenty of little golf course ponds. . . . My friend and I decided to go fishing. I rigged up a Flying Lure in the two-inch model. I cast out under some lily pads. Well, I kept on getting strikes, but I couldn't set the hook. Finally, BOOM! I had one. I reeled him in, "he" referring to a seventeen-inch largemouth bass.

Jim goes on to tell of another bass he caught on the same day and how the big one almost got away! Do you see what happened here? As he was fishing, Jim got plenty of strikes on the two-incher. After a while he got the hang of hooking them and was on his way to more successes in fishing.

I recently got a touching letter from Carolyn Platt about her husband, whom she describes as a novice fisherman. Here is the letter in its entirety.

> For a Christmas present, I got my husband a Flying Lure. We went to our summer home in the first weekend in May and took the lure. He sat down and opened the box for the first time and read the whole instructions very carefully. The next night, he was very tired from building a pier but decided to relax and try the lure. Less than ten minutes after he threw it out, a big fish bit.

The Hibdon family. *(Courtesy Guido Hibdon)*

Our neighbors were watching and one of them rushed over to help when [my husband] started yelling. The fish was going under the pier and he thought he was going to lose it. The line was a ten-pound line.

Other neighbors heard the splashing and came over with their cameras. They could not believe their eyes.

We called the taxidermist since it was Sunday night just before dark and he met us at his shop. His description of the largemouth bass was "Humongous." He weighed in at nine pounds.

The next morning, he went back on the pier [in our front yard] and within twenty minutes he had caught a three-pound bass before breakfast.

I have already gotten back more than the cost of the lure from seeing the look of excitement on his face.

My husband was sixty-five April 23 and is a novice fisherman. What a way to celebrate.

Fishing and the Family

I often tell people that fishing isn't all that important in the scheme of things . . . and they get perplexed. How could I, of all people, say that? The reason I say that is because how we relate to our friends and family is where the true value of fishing can lie—like the happiness and memories that Carolyn and her husband will have of his sixty-fifth birthday.

The Hibdons, Guido and Stella and Dion and his wife, are a great example of how fishing can bring a family together. Guido, who is a former world champion, and his son Dion, one of the top pros in the country, fish tournaments, travel, practice, and socialize together. Their family activities are based on the sport and they are drawn closer by it. What conflict between generations?

12

Putting It All Together

Case Study: Largemouth Bass in the Spring

To help you use the Flying Lure Success System, let's look at a case study of the largemouth bass, America's most popular game fish, during one season, the spring. As we follow the habits of this game fish throughout the season, you will see how to apply the concepts contained in the thirty-three Success Questions. Then you'll be ready to go out and tackle your own set of circumstances and fish species.

The "When" in Fishing

The most frequently repeated mistake I see happening in the pursuit of fish relates to *when* you are fishing. I call it the W.H.Y. Syndrome. W.H.Y. stands for "Were here yesterday."

The situation usually plays out like this. No matter where or when I am fishing a lake, I often spot a local fisherman who lives on the body of water. The local has been fishing the lake his whole life. He goes out at dawn and at dusk to the places where he has caught fish in the past. Usually he'll be fishing the shallowest, weediest bay he can find—no matter what time of year it is or what the weather is like. Most often he fishes with little or no success, day after day after day.

Why would any human being do this to him- or herself? Because people don't understand that *when* they are fishing determines *where* they should be fishing. This fisherman will have success only when the fish move to him! In shallow bays, this usually means only the spring and the fall. For the rest of the year, the fish aren't home—they're out on the town! They're behind you, laughing their tails off.

Successful fishermen move to where the fish are, based on the season, and don't wait for the fish to come to them.

Unfortunately, I understand these local fishermen all too well. In my early days of fishing I was one of them. The reason I kept fishing shallow bays all year was the memory of the huge fish I had seen and caught in those areas in the spring.

I remember an early spring morning many years ago, standing knee deep in water, fishing for largemouth bass. The water was still cold around my bare feet, but felt warmer toward the surface, due to a bright May sun. All of a sudden, I was startled by large shapes in the water moving slowly from the darkness of the deep water into the clear sandy cove where I stood. My heart leaped. Like a slow-moving freight train, a dark school of perhaps one hundred or more large bass was migrating into my little cove. At the head of the school were bass that weighed over twelve pounds—a state record at that time. As the procession swam by me, the bass got smaller: Ten pounds, eight pounds, six pounds, and finally about four pounds. To this day, I have never seen anything like this again. I was so shocked that by the time I regained my concentration, the school had almost swum by. I cast my nightcrawler to the rear of the school, and one of the smaller bass, about a four-pounder, darted out and grabbed the bait. On any other day, a four-pounder would have been a great accomplishment for this young fisherman, but not that day, not when I just saw the granddaddies of the lake lazily swim by as if I weren't even there.

The lesson here is that the season contains powerful forces that make fish behave and migrate to certain places. Like a magnet, the spring spawning cycle drew the bass out of deep water to the shallows to create nests and spawn. This is when most fishermen see big fish in shallow water. Yet just as quickly and powerfully as nature drew that school of bass into my shallow cove, it will draw them back out into deeper water. Sadly, the uneducated fisherman will live in the memory of the only big fish he's ever seen in the spring—and will continue to fish shallow areas without success, until the fish return next year.

Ironically, I believe that fishing has a psychologically addictive quality even in failure. Once in college I read a psychological study about addictive behaviors. Its premise was that addictive activities are generally those where success and failure is random and can't be predicted—like horse racing, the lottery, or alas, fishing without a clue of what you're doing.

My job is to put as many odds in your favor as possible through knowledge.

How the Season Affects Fishing

The world moves in seasonal cycles. Birds, fish, animals, and even we humans do. Birds fly north and south depending on the season. Even business cycles move on by season. We purchase cars and houses in the spring, we watch more TV in the fall and winter. Time and seasonality affect everyone.

Time and seasonality affect fish dramatically. Here I will be using the most popular game fish in the United States, the largemouth bass, to illustrate many of the formula's points. I will also discuss other species as we go along. Whatever species you are fishing for will fit into the fishing success formula.

Fish behave differently in each of the seasons. In the spring the primary urge of most warm-water fish is to spawn. Bass generally spawn in shallow water. In the summer the same fish seek to feed and maintain a safe place to exist, generally moving into deeper water.

Ah, spring . . . when the thoughts of young boys and girls turn to fancy, or fish. And when thoughts of fish turn toward, well, other fish. When does spring occur from the fish's point of view? That's the real question. Quite simply, it occurs when the water temperature rises to the one at which a particular species begins to spawn. I've actually simulated this event in an aquarium with tropical fish. By slowly raising the water temperature, you can fool fish into spawning no matter what time of the year it is. Sure, it's a rotten trick, but the fish didn't complain.

For a bass, the temperature range that begins the spawning cycle is around the low to mid-60s° F. I can't give an exact temperature because there isn't one. There are variations among geographical areas. There are even variations between lakes in a region. Why? Who knows? They just exist. I believe that fish in different ponds have developed slight genetic or behavioral variations.

What about "preferred temperature" charts that are published in books and magazines? Be skeptical. People tend to be very sure about what they don't know—especially experts.

Spring occurs as a sliding band across the United States, starting as

HOW SEASON AFFECTS THE WAY WE SHOULD FISH OR HOW *"WHEN"* AFFECTS THE 4 P'S

	SPRING	SUMMER	FALL	WINTER
PLACE	Shallow	Medium depth	Shallow and medium depth	Deep
PROXIMITY	Prespawn: Far Spawn: Very close	No cover: Far In cover: Close	Generally: Medium In cover: Close	Close
PRESENTATION	Prespawn: Medium speed Spawn: Slow speed	No cover: Fast speed In cover: Slow speed	Generally: Medium speed In cover: Slow speed	Slow speed
PERSISTENCE	Prespawn: Low Spawn: High	No cover: Medium In cover: High	Generally: High In cover: High	High

WHEN IS SPRING?

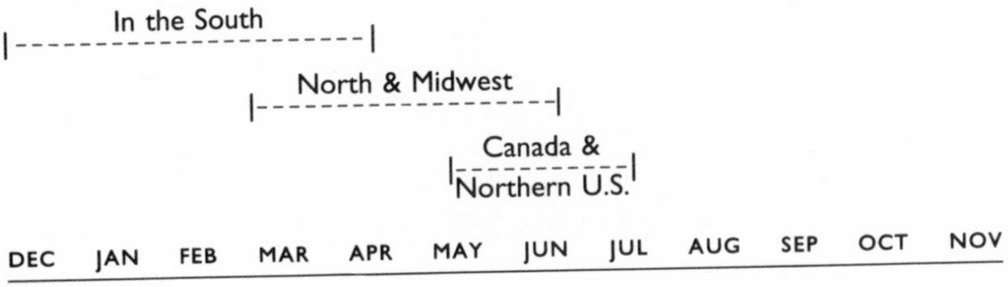

In the South: DEC – APR

North & Midwest: MAR – JUN

Canada & Northern U.S.: MAY – JUL

DEC JAN FEB MAR APR MAY JUN JUL AUG SEP OCT NOV

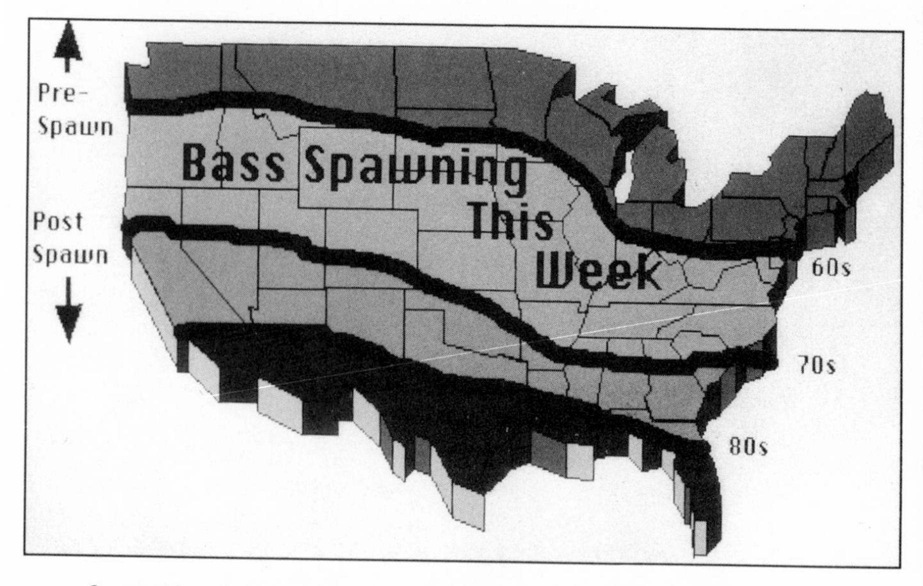

Seasonal bands move across the United States. *(Courtesy Alex Langer)*

early as December in Florida to as late as July in Maine and Canada. Picture the "Spawning Band" in the map, slowly sliding from south to north. This is spring. One spring weekend, as I was broadcasting my live radio show across the United States, a man called in to report spawning bass in Florida. A few minutes later another man called from Wisconsin to tell me about ice-fishing! The fish in Wisconsin may not be spawning for another five months. No wonder they're cranky.

Prespawn, Spawn, and Postspawn

From the fish's point of view—the only one that matters—spring is divided into three parts.

Prespawn is the time just before the spawn itself. Depending on the weather, the prespawn can last a few days or a few weeks. The prespawn can be some of the most phenomonal shallow-water fishing you'll ever experience. Big fish are actively patrolling and feeding in the vicinity of where they are about to spawn.

The spawn is the time the fish are actually making their nests, breeding, and protecting their spawn from intruders.

The post-spawn occurs when the fish are through spawing and move off the beds to rest and feed after their strenuous spawning period.

The Effect of Spring on the Four P's

PLACE

In natural lakes, the better places tend to be the shallow coves. You should focus especially on the northeast areas of a lake, since prevailing winds from the southwest tend to warm up the surface water and blow it in a northeasterly direction.

The best places tend to be shallow areas with a sandy bottom if it is available. Bass prefer to spawn on a sandy bottom because it is a bacteria-free area that can be guarded easily. Bass generally avoid weedy or mucky bottoms since they harbor bacteria and eggs are easily lost in the mess. Bass fan their eggs with their tails while they are on their beds to keep water circulating around them and to keep bacteria from settling on them.

Don't be fooled! Bottoms that look mucky and weedy sometimes have sand just under the muck. Bass will clear these areas with their tails when the spawn starts. Check out areas with lily pads. They often hide a sandy bottom covered by inches of leaves and muck.

Shallow Coves: The Warmest Water in a Lake (number 1 on map)

Fish will use the warmest water available in a lake to begin the spring spawn. The warmest water is found earliest in shallow cove areas for two reasons: (1) Shallow water is more easily heated than deep water, where heat dissipates; and (2) The coves are segregated from the rest of the lake and are generally protected from wind, which tends to disperse warm water.

Areas Near Inflows and Outflows (number 2 on map)

Inflows (streams running into a lake) often bring warmer water into a lake if they come from another smaller pond where they skim off warm surface water. Just such a situation occurred in the shallow cove where I had my first successes with big bass. A small stream filled the shallow cove with warm oxygenated water, which became a magnet to big bass. This water came from a smaller pond half a mile away. At the time, I just stumbled onto this goldmine. Now I look for these situations whenever I fish a new lake in the spring.

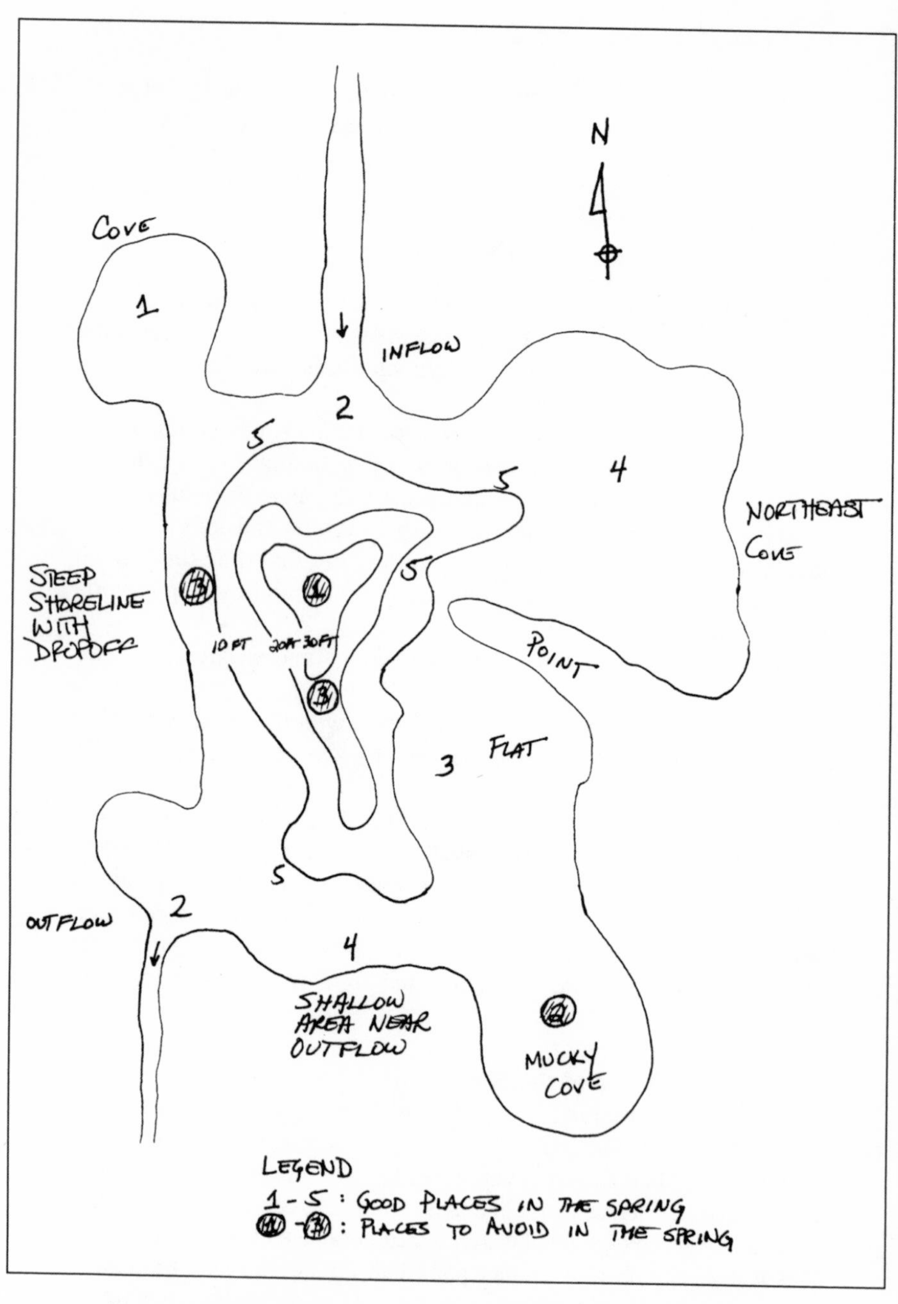

The best and worst places to fish in the spring. *(Courtesy Alex Langer)*

SUCCESS STORY

My fishing partner Ray Lentine and I won a team tournament on South Watuppa Pond, in Fall River, Massachusetts, by duplicating just such a situation in 1990. We were fishing a large cove with a major inflow. Ray and I were able to catch a string of nice bass as well as the lunker of the tournament. At the time, we knew it was a good spot with a warm-water inflow. It was only later that Ray discovered, by doing more research and getting a map of the area, that the inflow was actually fed by the warm water of a northeast cove from an adjacent lake that we never knew about! It's no wonder that spring tournaments have consistently been won in this area of South Watuppa Pond for decades.

Outflows are streams or rivers that take water out of a lake—they are the opposite of inflows. Outflows tend to draw warmer surface water to themselves, much like pouring gravy out of a pan. The top gravy pours out of the pan first—you are skimming the surface. In exactly the same way, an outflow skims and "vacuums" warm surface water toward itself. By doing so, it creates a shallow, warm, oxygenated area, if conditions are right. Fish will be drawn to the warmer water and will generally spawn earlier near an outflow.

Flats That Contain No Fish the Rest of the Year (number 3 on the map)
One of the biggest discoveries I made in spring fishing is that areas that are considered poor or foolish places to fish during the rest of the year can produce extraordinary catches—because they are overlooked.

MY SPRING HUMILITY LESSON

For years I fished for, and caught, large bass in the spring on one of my favorite lakes. One day I saw my friend Steve fishing hundreds of yards off shore. If it were anyone else, I would have dismissed him as an inexperienced fisherman and continued with my fishing. There are obviously no bass hundreds of yards off shore in the spring. Right? This bothered me because Steve was the best fisherman in this part of the country. Why would Steve be fishing in a "stupid" area? The answer: He wouldn't be.

We compared notes at the end of the day when we got back to the launch ramp. I did well, but Steve did better—twice as well, in fact. He had caught and released nearly twenty bass, including some lunkers. I had about eight fish that day—not bad, or so I thought. Why was Steve catching all those fish? Because he had found an overlooked area. There was a large offshore flat—a shallow sloping area that was sandy and devoid of fish all year . . . except in the spring. The same attributes that made it devoid of fish year round, sandy and shallow, made it an ideal spawning area for a few weeks during the year.

That flat continued to be the most productive springtime area for catching bass for years. Alas, over time our secret was discovered, and every spring we now have to compete with other fishermen for this prime turf. But the lesson is that there are many such areas that are overlooked when springtime bass should be on the shoreline. Find a sandy flat, and you may have weeks of prime bass fishing with absolutely no competition from shoreline beaters.

Any Shallow Area (number 4 on the map)

Don't overlook any shallow area that may not be productive during other times of the year, such as coves, flats, beaches, points, and so forth. Anyplace in a lake that is shallow will heat up quickly in the springtime sun. If it isn't a spawning area, it may be a staging area or a roaming area. You can often catch a single huge bass roaming, or foraging, during the prespawn and early spawn . . . and you may never catch another bass there again. Fish move great distances in the spring and could be in any shallow area. Believe it!

One more important point must be made about shallow-water fishing in the spring: Even though you may be fishing in one to three feet of water or less, you will usually not see the fish, even in crystal-clear water. Sure, you'll see some, but don't be lulled into a sense of security. *Not seeing a fish in shallow water doesn't mean it's not there.* There is a type of bass I have nicknamed a "sandbass." This fish seems to materialize out of nowhere, out of the sand bottom, if you will. You could be looking at a sandy bottom right next to the boat in twelve inches of water. You drop your lure in the water and a huge bass materializes out of nowhere and grabs it. This has happened to me time after time. Fish camouflage themselves so well that they are undetectable from the surface 99.9 percent of the time.

Staging Areas Near Shallow Areas (dropoffs and points) (number 5 on the map)
Any area near shallow spawning areas is a prime suspect for holding prespawning bass. During the spawn and prespawn, dropoffs and deeper areas near shallow water can hold fish and should be explored. Once you have located bass in a shallow area, fan out from it into adjacent deeper water if the action slows down.

THE WORST PLACES TO FISH IN THE SPRING

Deep Water (number 1 on the map)
Avoid deep water in the spring. The bass aren't there. They've gone to the big city to have a good time, and won't be back until the early summer.

Weedy or Mucky Bottom with No Rock or Sand Underneath It (number 2 on the map)
Avoid areas that look good but aren't. These are shallow areas with a silty or mucky bottom that has no sand or gravel underneath it to support a spawning bed. Fish may cruise through these areas and you may catch an occasional one, but don't camp here. Find the best areas with the hardest, cleanest bottom you can.

The Coldest Water in the Lake (number 3 on the map)
The coldest water will generally be on open, fast-dropping shorelines or in the southern part of a lake, where warm southern prevailing winds don't blow warm surface water to shore. Avoid these areas in the spring.

There are bad run-ins, where cold water runs into a lake, as opposed to good run-ins, which I discussed before, where warm water enters a lake. The bad run-ins look just like good run-ins except they are fed by cool mountain streams or underground streams and not a reservoir of warm water. The cool water retards the fishing and the progress of the spawn. The only way to distinguish between good and bad run-ins is with a temperature gauge. Spring is one of the few times of the year where a surface temperature gauge is indispensable.

Even a few degrees of difference between one cove and another can mean the difference between fish and no fish. I remember one recent spring trip where coves that were at 62° F. had hot fishing. Coves that were 60° F. or less were dead.

PROXIMITY

Proximity is a new concept which I introduced with the advent of the Flying Lure. It helps anglers think about the fishing situation in a unique way. Anglers should ask themselves, "How close to the fish should my lure to be today?" and "Are the fish holding tight to cover, or are they roaming around?" Proximity considers two questions:

1. How close to the fish must the lure be to be effective on a given day? (Two inches? Two feet? Two yards?) How far will a fish move to strike a lure?
2. What type of cover will a fish be close to on a given day?

For example, during the spawn, the types of cover that fish will be near are shallow bottom obstructions, such as sunken trees, stumps, tires, shopping carts, and anything else that provides shade or cover. Fish will build a nest right next to these obstructions and will remain very close to the nest, seldom venturing more than a few feet away. In this case, during the spawn, proximity works in two ways: The lure must be presented to the fish very close and the fish remains very close to the surrounding cover.

The pinpoint proximity required of the lure explains why the Flying Lure has been used with such great success in the spring by fishermen all over the country.

SUCCESS STORY
LAKE RECORD CAPTURED IN THE SPRING
OR BOY WHO CRIED "BASS"

One of the greatest thrills I get as a lure inventor is when people use my creations to catch true trophy fish. I got a call in February 1992 from Norman Sanders, the owner of Smoothy's Sport Tackle, a fishing store in Abilene, Texas. Norman introduced himself and proceeded to tell me that one of his customers, Dean Goodman, just caught a lake record bass on the Flying Lure. The bass weighed over twelve pounds! Needless to say, I was so excited that I immediately called Dean myself. His story, which he later related on my radio show and on national television, was amazing.

Dean and his son Kevin went fishing on a February morning on Clyde Lake in Texas. It was a cloudy day with some early drizzle. Father and son caught nothing. On the way home, Kevin called his mother from Dean's cellular phone and told her they caught a lake record bass . . . and Mom hung up because they were pulling her leg.

In the afternoon, the sun had come out, and the Goodmans decided to go out on the lake again. Bass were in an early spawning condition. There was sunken brush everywhere in the shallow water. Dean was throwing a six-inch chartreuse Flying Lure close to the sunken obstructions. Both father and son started catching some small fish. The water level was up a few feet over normal. (Clyde Lake is actually a small man-made reservoir with a dam, which can make water levels fluctuate.) Dean saw a sunken willow tree sticking out of the water and pitched the lure right beside it. Dean specifically did not cast the lure in the usual overhand manner, but "flipped" it in a short underhand motion. Short, accurate casts of ten to thirty feet are the way to fish when fish are holding tight to cover. There's no reason to make long, arcing casts, unless the water is crystal clear and the fish are easily spooked.

Dean's cast landed next to one side of the tree. He let the lure swim away from him, into the limbs of the tree. Dean related, "Once the lure had traveled a few feet, it stopped. Then it shot out of the tree like a rocket. I set the hook and immediately knew I had a big fish on." At that moment Dean screamed at Kevin to get the net. At first, Kevin wouldn't do it, saying "That isn't a big fish." But Dean insisted, so Kevin grabbed the net while Dean was wrestling with the fish, still on his line.

Then Kevin looked down beside the boat, and the biggest fish mouth he had ever seen was scowling out of the water at him. He was so startled that he dropped the net and ran to the back of the boat! "I can't tell you what he said when he saw that fish!" Dean later recalled.

After the ordeal, Dean and Kevin had the fish officially weighed and certified by the Texas Department of Wildlife. At 12.06 pounds, it was an official lake record at that time.

On the way home, Kevin called his mother again and told her that his father had caught a lake record. As usual, she hung up the phone. When they got home, Dean and Kevin went into the house and insisted that Mrs. Goodman go outside to look at the fish, which was in the boat. She refused to go outside until Dean pleaded with her. By then neighbors had gathered around the boat to see the huge fish. Video cameras were rolling and pictures were being snapped. Father and son were heroes.

Smoothy's store now has a large mural painted on the outside wall with a leaping bass—and hooked in the side of its mouth is, you guessed it, a chartreuse Flying Lure, just like the one Dean used to catch his record. In the local paper, the sports headline read NEW LURE HELPS CATCH CLYDE LAKE RECORD.

Why were Dean and Kevin successful? They were fishing in the right *place,* shallow warmer water. They were in the *proximity* of shallow bottom cover that holds fish tightly during that time of the year. Their lure was pitched tightly in the proximity of the fish and swam even tighter into the cover because it had the ability to "fly" forward underwater. They put together the variables—when, place, and proximity—and came out WINNERS! Will the fish still be in the same place in July? Probably not!

PRESENTATION

Presentation means the type of offering you're going to throw at the fish on a particular day. This includes the speed of your lure, its color, its size, and its type of action. Generally, different presentations are required during prespawn, spawn, and postspawn.

Dean Goodman and his son Kevin with a 12.06-pound lake record largemouth bass. *(Courtesy Sandra Bruton)*

Prespawn Presentation

During the prespawn, fish are roaming and actively feeding more of the time than during other parts of the year. They are stocking up with food in preparation for the spawn, when they may not eat for days or weeks. During this time your presentation should cover as much water as possible. The fish are roaming. You should be too. Don't camp in one shallow area, unless you know it to be an exceptional spawning area. Even so, you should still keep moving to strain as much water as possible. During the prespawn it's a numbers game. No shallow area should be overlooked.

During the prespawn, you should also be trying to match the food color and size found in that body of water at that time. If it is shad, then use a shad-colored lure. If the predominant food fish is yellow perch, go for a lure with yellows and greens in it. Also, try to match the approximate size of the quarry at that time of year. If the quarry is a small fish of four to six inches, use lures of that general size.

What type of lure, then, should you select for the prespawn? Spinnerbaits are an excellent choice, because they can be used to cover water quickly. Again, if the food fish is silvery, like the shad, try to use silver blades and a skirt in the white/black/silver family. If the food fish is perch or bream, use copper blades and skirts that generally match the color pattern of the food fish. It doesn't have to be exact. Don't be too picky.

A Flying Lure spinnerbait is my personal choice during the prespawn because it is made for shallow-water fishing. Its "wing" keeps the lure shallow and allows it to ride over obstructions of the worst kind unmolested. However, if you need the lure to have some persistence with a following fish, you can give the lure some slack line and it will drop back right into that fish's face.

Shallow-running crankbaits (of the one- to five-foot variety) are also a good alternative. Again, match those colors to the food fish whenever possible. You can cover lots of ground with crankbaits, and the fishing during this time of the year is often not finesse. I prefer floating crankbaits at this time, since you're fishing shallow water and want to see them come up when you stop the retrieve—not get snagged on the bottom.

Cast your spinnerbaits and crankbaits around obstructions, but don't be hung up on finding them. Unlike any other time of the year, the fish are roaming and could be in shallow, open water anywhere you cast. Work spinnerbaits at a steady, medium speed. If you bump one over an obstruction, slow it down and probe what's down there. Let the spinnerbait flutter down to the bottom. If you feel a hit, set the hook immediately. Many of my bigger bass in the spring and fall have come on spinnerbaits that have bumped into some debris on the bottom (that I didn't know about) that happened to hold a big fish.

If you find an interesting underwater hang-up with the spinnerbait, cast a Flying Lure down there to probe it further and more thoroughly.

Always remember, your mission at this time of the year is to cover and strain as much water as possible. Imagine your many casts as the web of the strainer or a stand of a big net. The bigger your net, the better your chances of bumping into a fish. Fish will chase and hit your lure at this time of the year like no other. Enjoy it.

You can use a Flying Lure quickly during the prespawn. Work it just under the surface of the water, almost like a Rattletrap lipless crankbait. Some people put glass rattles inside the body cavity of the Flying Lure to give it more sound during its retrieve. The beauty of using the Flying Lure in this way is that you can stop it on a dime and make it change

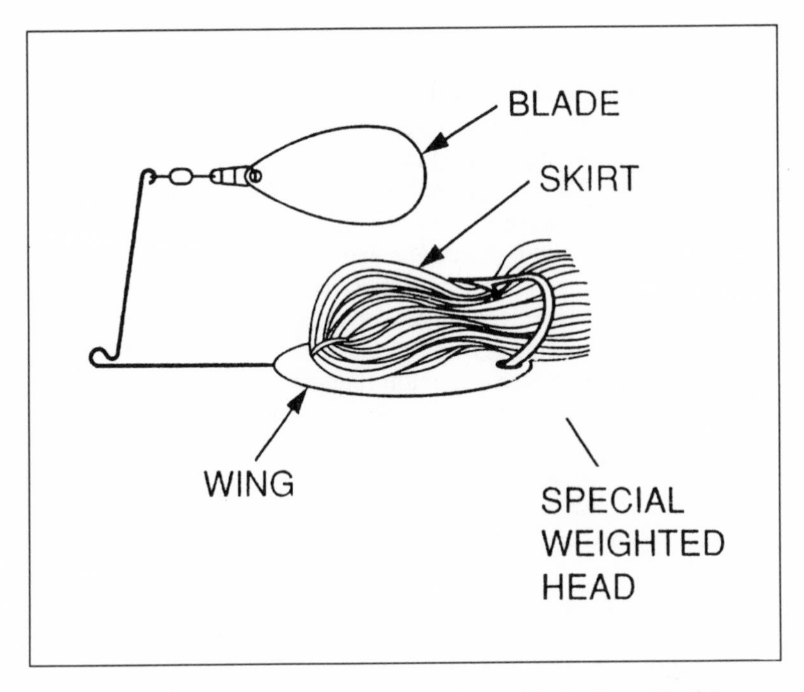

Flying Lure spinnerbait. Flash and vibration along with the "punch" of the Flying Lure action. The spinnerbait's flat body is made of soft plastic, so fish hold on—just like the original Flying Lure. *(Courtesy Alex Langer)*

direction to trigger a strike. When I come to a cove that I know to be, or suspect of being, a good spawning area, I'll use the Flying Lure.

The prespawn can be the easiest fishing available. This is the time that most local fishermen make their "catch of the year," without a clue as to why they caught it. The reason: fish are shallow, accessible, and feeding—not a bad combination if you can find it!

The prespawn is about the only time of the year that the persistence of a lure isn't that important because the bass are so aggressive. Aggressive bass will simply attack your lure and ask questions later; they usually don't need to be coaxed. Just about any lure that can effectively cover water is capable of catching a fish during this time. But, in my experience, a persistent and naturally presented soft plastic Flying Lure often attracts the bigger fish during the prespawn.

Presentation During the Spawn

After the frenzy of the prespawn, the landscape changes dramatically. Fish mostly stop feeding and begin to play house. Uh-oh, you might say, we're in trouble! Well, not really. Although a fish's motivations may change, we can still make it strike a lure, but for different reasons. At this point, put away your crankbaits and spinnerbaits. It's a new day.

Fish are spawning on their fanned-out nests a few feet in diameter. If you don't invade their space, you won't catch a fish. It's that clear cut. You should be using Flying Lures or jigs to invade their world.

Color often doesn't much matter during the spawn. Accuracy of lure placement is 99 percent of the game. So is *persistence,* which a few days ago, during prespawn, didn't matter as much.

You must learn how to spot spawning beds. In dirty water, it's nearly impossible. In these cases I suggest straining the water with a slow-rolling spinnerbait or a larger-size (six-inch) Flying Lure. Cast near visible obstructions, which often have a nest beside them.

In clear water—and thankfully, most fresh water is generally clear in the spring—you can visually spot spawning beds as patches of yellow sand or light rock. You must wear polarized glasses when fishing for spawning fish or you'll miss most of your opportunities. You are trying to spot beds and then cast to them without spooking the fish by running your boat too close to them. Polarized glasses cut down the glare from the water and let you spot beds much farther away than with the naked eye. If you've never spotted beds before, doing so will take a little practice. The appearance of beds will vary from lake to lake. They generally look like white china dishes in the water. Once you get the hang of it, you'll be able to tell a bed from a rock from a sand patch, just by seeing the hue of the water reflecting up from the object. It's a fun way to fish.

Cast your lure past the bed, and then bring your lure back to the boat, bumping along the bottom, until it is actually in the spawning bed itself. Here persistence is the key. The longer you keep it in the bed, the more of a chance the lure will have of being struck by an angry bass that wants to kill it and clear it from the nest.

The beauty of the Flying Lure is that you can continually tease the fish on the nest. For the first five casts with a conventional lure, a bass may have no interest in the invader. Without recasting multiple times, you can make the Flying Lure constantly swim back into the nest, until you elicit a strike. In fishing for smallmouth bass on the beds, you sometimes get the feeling that the fish will never attack, as it sits motionless, looking at your bait. Every time you let the lure go back into the nest after pulling it out about a foot, you get a little more equity in that fish. After six to ten pulls, that equity pays off, and the fish attacks. Have patience. It works. But remember, try to release spawning fish right away, where you caught them.

Presentation During the Postspawn

Postspawn is the time after the fish leave their nests and before they fall into their summer feeding patterns. It can be some of the worst fishing of the year! And that's just weeks after some of the best fishing has occurred. Nature plays its tricks on us! If we don't respond, we'll be wasting our time.

How do we fish for postspawning fish? After the spawn, many of the bass that have just mated are languishing near the areas of the spawn, around stumps, weed beds, and dropoffs. They are tired and recuperating. Some of these fish literally look dazed. Consider that salmon die after spawning. Although bass survive, they have undergone a very strenuous period, perhaps the most stress-producing time in their lives. They need a rest.

Some lakes are almost impossible to fish during the postspawn. Some larger lakes are not bad since not all bass spawn at the same time. While some bass are in postspawn, others are still spawning. You can fish during the postspawn, but results can be hit or miss.

A recent BASS tournament at Lake Murray in Columbia, South Carolina, produced record catches during a postspawn period. What's the reason? First, Lake Murray is an excellent, fertile lake with a large and heavy bass population. Second, not all bass were off the spawn yet. Many were still spawning, because Lake Murray is a huge reservoir with multiple conditions occurring at the same time. While some bass were finished spawning, others were still on the spawn.

To fish postspawn effectively (and effective is a relative term here), you should cover a lot of water, using slow-moving lures such as soft plastics and jigs. You must try to find the more active members of a sluggish clan of fish. But although you should cover a lot of water, the fish generally prefer a more slowly moving bait. Make lots of pinpoint casts with a Flying Lure. Keep your lure in place for a short time, near cover or near a dropoff. Be persistent, but move on if a few casts in an area have not paid off. If you stay in one place, you'll often get very frustrated fishing for the same inactive fish over and over.

PERSISTENCE
During the prespawn period persistence is less important than usual because fish are actively roaming and feeding. Here, other strike triggers, such as natural swimming action and change in lure direction, are the key.

The *persistence* in the spring is at its height when bass are on the beds. If your lure doesn't tease that fish as well as invade its nesting space, it may not hit it. A persistent lure on a spawning bed is as close to a sure thing as I've ever seen.

After the spawn and before the summer, persistence is very important as well. Fish are often extremely unaggressive and must be coaxed tirelessly into striking a lure—and very close to cover and weeds.

By integrating the information you will get by answering the thirty-three Fishing Success Questions, as we have just done here, you can now analyze other fishing seasons in the same way this one has been analyzed. It's an exciting challenge!

Some Final Tips

Be a student of fishing. Never stop learning. Always ask questions of others and of yourself. Always be ready to determine "What's really happening here?" no matter how much energy that takes.

Keep Learning

A small number of pioneering magazines have developed the modern body of knowledge that we call fishing. To keep learning, you must keep fishing and reading and listening to others who can help sharpen your knowledge and inquisitive skills.

The late Jason Lucas of *Sports Afield* magazine and Bill Plummer were among those who began modern American fishing after World War II. They and others like Gadabout Gaddis were the pioneers in the field.

Ray Scott and the writers and editors of *BASSMASTER* have exemplified the inquisitive knowledge gathering that makes tournament winners just that, winners. They put forth facts that work, whether there is a theory behind it or not. Likewise, Al and Ron Lindner publish an excellent instructional magazine called *In Fisherman* and they have kept pushing forward the limits of structure fishing to new heights. *Fishing Facts* magazine, the originator of structure fishing, keeps presenting intelligent articles that help expand our horizons. Use all of these magazines to gain knowledge, and yet be critical and questioning in your thinking. Always go back to the thirty-three Fishing Success Questions.

Hal Lyman and Frank Woolner, the original publisher and editor of *Saltwater Sportsman* magazine, did for saltwater fishing what *BASSMASTER* did for bass fishing—they started an industry and a popularized sport. Keep putting good knowledge into your mind by reading these magazines and other reality-based fishing research and articles. And remember to look at everything critically. Trust your instincts when you start to apply this knowledge on the water. If it doesn't work, try something else. Keep changing and experimenting!

There are also a number of excellent fishing TV programs that teach as well as entertain. These include Don Meissner's *Rod and Reel Streamside,* seen on public television stations, Jerry McKinnis's program, *The Fishin' Hole,* on ESPN, and Hank Parker's *Outdoor* magazine on TNN. Of course, the Flying Lure infomercials will continue to air to keep the "Flying Lure Family" apprised of news, products, or anything else that happens in the Flying Lure realm.

For real-time fishing discussions and news, you can tune in to my own radio program, *Fishing Live!* heard on the American Sports Radio Network nationwide, to talk and exchange information with fishermen from around the country. What's the point of all this? Simply that you should stay in touch with other fishermen and keep informed. Fishing often changes rapidly, and you can benefit from staying in touch with these changes, in products, techniques, or scientific discoveries about fish behavior. Fishing is very much an evolving science. You can study it all your life and still not know everything there is to know. I am convinced that we don't know more about fishing than we do know. That's exciting. There are opportunities to learn and discover at every turn.

In fishing there are often more questions than answers. Ask the right questions, and you *will* succeed.

Above all, *have fun!* People, friends, and family are what's important. That's the real lesson of fishing. Nothing else.

See you on the water!

FREE OFFER

For a free hook to accompany the Flying Lure enclosed in this book, please send:

A stamped, self addressed envelope

TO:

The Flying Lure
P.O. Box 755
Hyde Park, MA 02136

For more information, or if you have photos, videotapes, or letters of your catches with the Flying Lure, please write to the above address.